BLUEPRINT FOR DIVERSITY

LAYING THE FOUNDATION FOR SUCCESS

DR. VERNON D. FRANKLIN

urbanpress

Blueprint for Diversity
by Dr. Vernon D. Franklin
Copyright © 2022 Dr. Vernon D. Franklin

ISBN 978-1-63360-201-4

For Worldwide Distribution
Printed in the U.S.A.

Urban Press
P.O. Box 8881
Pittsburgh, PA 15221-0881
412.646.2780

TABLE OF CONTENTS

DEDICATION

The words of my uncle spoken to me in my adolescence still ring loud and clear in my mind: "What you do speaks so loud, I can't hear what you say." My uncle's words of wisdom are appropriate in the dedication of this book to all staff who faithfully serve institutions while experiencing the empty words of appreciation for their service. Those words rang hollow because they have felt invisible, were never championed for their potential, or felt less valued because of their race, gender, or disability. You know who you are.

Also, it extends to you who heard the call for social justice from institutions when Mr. George Floyd was murdered in 2020 while at the same time feeling the knee of institutional injustice on your neck as you recalled painful infractions of exclusion that also left you breathless. Despite feeling under-appreciated in your workplace, you remained committed to an institution with a shortsighted vision that could see social injustice far outside their institution but not within its walls. You are the unsung heroes in those institutions who show up every day, give your best service, and bring your authentic self to institutions that espouse an inclusion and diversity vision but do not fully embrace you or see your potential.

Imagine how institutions and organizations would function without dedicated support staff like you. Robert Greenleaf (1991), pioneer of servant leadership concepts, focused on a fictional character named Leo, who embodied Greenleaf's concepts of servant leadership. While on a journey, Leo's dedicated service keeps the campsite well organized for his fellow nomadic campers. The impact of Leo's service went unnoticed until his mysterious disappearance left the encampment in disarray. Later, the travelers found that Leo was the head of a monastery, but he had displayed the aspects of servant leadership so well that his fellow travelers only saw the servant and missed the fact that he was the leader—the true leader among them, even though he did not carry the title. That is how you have been—and I have been among you as well.

Hypothetically, if organizational support staff would not show up with their best service, it would create a similar scenario as Leo's sudden departure. If these organizations could discover the unrecognized potential of their staff, imagine the untapped synergy and productivity that would then galvanize workplace advancement, resulting in a culture where diversity and inclusion would no longer be fading echoes but would provide evidence of tangible Inclusion and Diversity Transformation. (I will refer to this term as ID Transformation throughout the remainder of this book.)

SPECIAL
DEDICATION
AND ACKNOWLEDGMENT

I am writing this book because Jinx Walton, the former Chief Information Officer for IT at the University of Pittsburgh, saw potential in me and offered me the Diversity and Inclusion Program Manager position for Pitt IT. Thus, my attempt to develop an inclusive department that embraces diversity was the impetus for Blueprint for Diversity. Jinx demonstrated transformational leadership and gave me professional opportunities that contributed to faculty, staff, and student learning and development within the university community.

My colleague, Jacqueline Huggins-Hill, exemplifies ID Transformation. She touched numerous individuals through her encouraging and supportive efforts during my tenure in higher education. In the dedication, I mentioned Robert Greenleaf's fictional character, Leo, who represented servant leadership. Leo demonstrated leadership that was not necessarily positional but instead emanated from stewardship. He saw others' needs as a calling to serve, and Jacqueline is such a woman.

Countless individuals have benefited from Jacqueline's unselfish service to help and provide guidance. Over two decades as a colleague, Jacqueline was my confidante and advisor. She encouraged me to bring out the hidden potential I didn't see in myself. I was not the only recipient of her intuition that caused her to see a need and provide encouragement and help. She is a phenomenal woman of grace who walks in the influence that transforms hearts. Special thanks to you, Jacqueline, one of my greatest life cheerleaders. It is an honor to acknowledge you in my book.

ABOUT THE AUTHOR

A Purposeful Life

Taken from Ritchie, 2011. A Purposeful life. *Pitt Chronicle*: https://www.chronicle.pitt.edu/story/ black-history-month-featurevernon-franklin-purposeful-life

Dr. Vernon Franklin, a Diversity and Inclusion Program Manager and Computer Trainer within Pitt's Computing Services and Systems Development (CSSD), has been working at the University of Pittsburgh for over three decades. Though he has held multiple positions at Pitt since he began in 1981, Franklin says his true passion is personal and professional development—helping individuals identify and pursue the purposes of lives well lived.

Franklin says, he came to understand that his own purpose was to help others find theirs. "Mentoring individuals is my whole life," he says. "Friends and family members have always sought me out for advice."

Leading weekly training sessions during Pitt's Human Resources orientation sessions for new hires is just one of the many ways that Franklin provides computer guidance to Pitt employees. He also trains faculty, staff, and students on new software when the University upgrades technology.

The biggest challenge as a computer trainer is the need to continually learn new technologies," says Franklin. "But once I get an understanding of a new technology, I can teach it. After I receive training on new software from our vendors, I develop our custom tools and training manuals."

Unbeknownst to Franklin when he was an undergraduate at Geneva College, an elective course in computers would set his future path. A sociology major, Franklin liked the computer class and decided to pursue a minor in business data processing. He received his bachelor's degree in sociology in 1976 and returned to Geneva for his master's degree in organizational leadership, which he received in 2000. Also, in 2018 he received a doctor of education from the University of Pittsburgh.

At Pitt, Franklin is highly regarded, particularly by his CSSD colleagues. Communications supervisor Orr Goehring has worked with Franklin since 2004 and said that he is an exemplary representative of the department at orientation sessions across campus. "I can't think of anyone better than Vernon to be the first point of contact from our department," says Goehring. "He's approachable and knowledgeable. He's a great trainer and meticulous in his preparation."

When asked to describe his greatest success at Pitt, Franklin answered without hesitation, "The greatest successes are when people leave my classes empowered. Many people have told me that I have a teaching style that is very patient and very thorough." Working in academic computing has put Franklin in touch with many students throughout the years. He said he's taken many young students under his wing and helped them set and reach their goals.

Tyler Karns (A&S '08) is one Pitt graduate who has benefited from a friendship with Franklin. The two met when Karns was a student worker for CSSD in 2005. "He has been a mentor to me," says Karns. "He makes me think about how I can better myself as a person—how I live my life. We have some very deep conversations about what is going on in our lives and what we can do to better ourselves."

Jackie Huggins (A&S '95), a communications specialist technical coordinator in CSSD, has worked with Franklin for 13 years and calls him her mentor. Huggins says Franklin has often helped her with her own personal and professional development and attributes many of her training skills to him. "I didn't have a strong teaching background, but I had a background in information technology. Vernon helped me bridge the gap between knowing my subject and actually communicating and teaching it to someone else," Huggins explained.

"Vernon can help you see a different perspective on things," she adds. "He has also helped me to recognize some of my own strengths. He sheds light on a lot of things professionally."

Franklin has found many opportunities to pursue his interest in personal and professional development at his church, Allegheny Center Alliance Church (ACAC) on Pittsburgh's North Side. In addition to serving on the board of elders and as a lay counselor, he has, for nearly eight years, led a life-purpose course. "We look at personality type, passion, talents, spiritual gifts, and life-shaping experiences to see how a person is wired and how God has equipped us as individuals," says Franklin. "We try to match people with their life purpose, life profession, or life ministry."

Franklin's desire to work within the church can be traced to his upbringing. His grandparents founded Pittsburgh's Victory Baptist Church, which began in his grandmother's home. Growing up, he was often asked to volunteer with the church. As an adult, Franklin pursued formal ministerial training. In 2002, he received a certificate in biblical counseling from Christian Research and Development, a ministerial training program based in Philadelphia, and he studied urban ministry at Pittsburgh Theological Seminary in 1998.

Through ACAC, Franklin also served as the coordinator for Aftercare Ministry, an inmate release program offered through the Allegheny County Jail. The program provides a place for people recently released from jail to be mentored and receive assistance finding housing, transportation, and jobs. The program allowed Franklin and the other mentors to meet once a week with former inmates. "We went over life skills and also had Bible lessons," says Franklin.

Franklin seems to have an endless supply of energy. When he is not offering training at Pitt and doing community work with his church, he can be found running in Highland Park before dawn; baking a variety of cakes, cookies, and breads; and experimenting with vegetarian cooking. And because he loves teaching, he also finds time to lead computer courses as an adjunct faculty member at the Community College of Allegheny County.

With his many commitments and activities, it's a wonder that Franklin's momentum never seems to flag. "Helping others motivates me. That is one of my gifts—when I'm able to be of service."

PREFACE

"No one pours new wine into old wineskins. Otherwise, the new wine will burst the skins; the wine will run out, and the wineskins will be ruined."
—Mark 2:22 (Ancient Parable)

Is your institution pouring new wine into old wineskins? When organizations try to implement a diversity program, that is often exactly what they are doing. In the analogy, the acidity of the new wine is too much for the worn wineskin to handle. The skins burst and the wine is wasted. Without an awareness of organizational realities, without knowing the principles of transformational leadership and the arduous task of staff preparation, by not planning with empathy and sustainability in mind, organizations are pouring the new wine of inclusion and diversity (ID) Transformation into old wineskins of institutional traditions that work against a sense of belonging. Since ID Transformation is referred to throughout this book, it is appropriate to provide a definition for clarity.

Diversity and *inclusion* have become the standard terminology for organizational programs to foster greater equity and fairness for marginalized people groups. But I would suggest we reverse the order because inclusion must be established *before* diversity can be embraced. That's the reason that from this point forward, I will be referring to ID. Thus, I am defining ID Transformation as *relationally-interconnected individuals who create a palpable sense of belonging that increases human and organizational capacity for progressive innovation.* I describe what ignites *ID Transformation* as the imagination from and experimentation with different and growing mindsets collaborating through their thoughts and talents. When there is a lack of understanding of the historic racial and gender biases embedded in the system of an institution, it prevents diversity, equity, and inclusion initiatives from being implemented effectively.

When interviewing a patient with psychological issues, the therapist does not analyze the symptoms before understanding the patient's historical causal effects. The same approach is necessary when implementing diversity initiatives in an organization with unresolved or unrecognized cultural issues that have gone unaddressed for decades. To cultivate an ID Transformational culture, leaders must first understand the culture and the consequent need for leadership development and staff preparation for change.

To facilitate that process for those interested, I introduce five building blocks in this book that provide practical preconditions to guide institutions as they develop an ID Transformational culture. They are:

1. organizational awareness

2. transformational leadership

3. staff preparation

4. empathetic planning

5. sustainability

When applied, these building blocks facilitate efforts that embrace diverse staff backgrounds by way of intentional efforts to collaborate and grow through a sense of belonging.

Unmet or unsuccessful outcomes towards establishing a diversity program are inevitable when stagnant mindsets are part of a workplace that is not open to ID practices. Therefore, leaders must be strategic in creating a sustainable learning culture that proves to be adaptive to change. An effective strategic plan for implementing a diversity program must ensure that best practices will become an integral part of the culture while also aligning with the institutional mission.

Societal norms are evolving at an astounding pace in the twenty-first century, which impacts every organization's mission. Thus, institutions must adapt to ever-changing trends by intentionally creating a culture that values diverse ideas from different people groups who connect and support the institutional mission. The discourse surrounding diversity within American organizations reveals that many organizations have a diverse clientele base but lack a diverse workforce. One reason for the scarcity of diversity within many institutions is the consequence of historical systemic biases related to race, gender, and disability within the organizational culture.

When inequalities within an institution's worldview go unchallenged, the status quo continues within its culture. The diversity disparity within many institutions is a paradox because institutions are considered progressive visionaries for society. Institutions have a wonderful opportunity to be societal models that provide evidence of diversity, equity, and inclusion throughout their culture that strengthens its human capacity.

Before a building contractor starts a construction project, an assessment of resources needed and land preparation are conducted. The same preconditions are essential before implementing a diversity program for institutions. In other words, an evaluation of the culture is crucial. The efforts to understand an institution's culture undergird the work towards an ideal culture of belonging, resulting in significant diversity benchmarks that will strengthen the institution's presence in society.

The five building blocks I introduce in this book are preconditions to the emergence of ID Transformational practices through the intentional and collaborative efforts of leaders and staff as together they grow. ID Transformational initiatives are adaptive challenges that generate change and will lead to new ways of thinking, increases in productivity, and the creation of a relevant and sustainable culture. The book consists of the following outline.

In the Introduction, I will provide insight into my motivation for writing this book and reference my professional and educational credentials. I also give a glimpse into my life-shaping experiences that created the lens through which I comprehend and advocate for ID Transformation within institutions.

This section includes my explanation of how ID Transformation fosters collaboration, productivity, and innovation in the workplace, resulting in new ways of thinking through a synergistic culture of belonging and interdependency. The

Introduction ends as I present a critical thinking exercise for reflective journaling to help you identify your life-shaping experiences that are influencing your interpretation of diversity.

Part One: Foundation for ID Transformation

Part One consists of two chapters describing the elements that support my building blocks for ID Transformation. Chapter One provides an overview of institutional adaptive challenges because of historical ideologies that impede new ways of thinking. The chapter also addresses good decision-making dynamics for a diversity program. It concludes with a critical-thinking exercise that examines a technical and adaptive challenge regarding decision making for a diversity program.

Chapter Two then describes the importance of institutional vision, explaining the importance of having a unified vision when establishing a stable foundation for the building blocks. I put forth two critical components for vision, which are *brand* and *charter*—the core concepts for a diversity program. A *brand* provides a unified meaning and a *charter* establishes standards that guide an institution's diversity program. The chapter ends with a critical-thinking exercise to guide you through the construction of both a brand and charter appropriate for your diversity program.

Part Two: Building Blocks for ID Transformation

In Part Two, I present the five building blocks for ID Transformation that institutions can use when creating diversity programs. Each building block contains two chapters describing a component that makes up the building block.

Building Block One: Organizational Awareness

In "Chapter Three: Culture," I discuss the culture's component for the building block of organizational awareness. The chapter provides the reasons why institutions must first clearly understand their culture relative to diversity. I examine culture with the help of Edgar Schein's components of organizational culture: artifacts, espoused values, and underlying assumptions. The chapter concludes with a critical-thinking exercise comprised of questions to identify Schein's components in your organization, while also helping you recognize cultural disconnects that hinder a sustainable diversity program.

In "Chapter Four: Accountability," I present the accountability component for the building block of organizational awareness. This component defines how to evaluate, improve, and assess ID outcomes within an organizational culture. For example, the accreditation standards for a higher education institution provide a grid that evaluates and assesses the evidence for an institution's student learning outcomes. When organizations implement diversity programs, they should use a similar accountability process to validate cultural ID Transformation efforts. This chapter ends with a critical-thinking exercise to show organizations how to create an accountability mechanism for their diversity program unique to their culture.

Building Block Two: Transformational Leadership

In "Chapter Five: Influence," I provide information about the influence component for the building block of transformational leadership. The chapter outlines the characteristics of a transformational leader. This leadership type is crucial if a culture seeks transformation as its end result. Quite simply, a diversity program will not have a lasting influence on its organization without transformational leaders. The chapter concludes with an exercise for the reader to evaluate their organization's leadership to be consistent with a rating scale for the four transformational leadership characteristics.

In "Chapter Six: Worldview," I illustrate the worldview component for the building block of transformational leadership. This component is a process for managers and supervisors to determine their worldview and what changes may be needed to adjust or broaden it. I developed this from my personal experiences with staff who often reported that their managers and supervisors had blind spots preventing them from understanding different cultural backgrounds. The chapter closes with an exercise that guides managers and supervisors through an action plan that will help broaden their worldview.

Building Block Three: Staff Preparation

In "Chapter Seven: Purpose," I explain the importance

of the purpose components for building block staff preparation. This chapter describes why knowing one's life purpose is crucial for staff preparation. Not knowing one's purpose limits anyone's professional contribution to an organization along with their professional and organizational advancement. The chapter concludes with an exercise that guides staff through the process of discovering their life purpose and its professional implications.

In "Chapter Eight: Advancement," I discuss the advancement component for building block staff preparation. The chapter describes an accountability process to assist staff in developing a continuous and personalized learning and development plan. This plan provides the means by which managers and supervisors can assist staff in planning a professional trajectory that benefits staff while also contributing to institutional advancement. The chapter ends with an exercise to guide leaders and staff in a collaborative effort that identifies professional development goals consistent with the institutional mission.

Building Block Four: Empathetic Planning

In "Chapter Nine: Strategy," I discuss the significance of the strategy component for the building block of empathetic planning. This component illustrates an organizational process to identify efficiencies or deficiencies in a diversity program. The chapter also shows the impact from organizational practices that will result in either a good or bad outcome where a cultural sense of belonging in concerned. I conclude this chapter with an exercise that highlights outcomes while developing a diversity program. Of course, the goal is to avoid negative actions that create barriers preventing positive organizational outcomes.

In "Chapter Ten: Collaboration," I discuss the collaboration component for the empathetic planning building block. The chapter discusses the importance of a shared partnership process among leaders and staff from diverse backgrounds to implement a diversity program. One of my recommendations is identifying an inclusion team that oversees administration and staff engagement programs to create a culture of belonging. This chapter once again concludes with an exercise to explain how an organization can use the collaboration component to create an inclusion team for its diversity program.

Building Block Five: Sustainability

In "Chapter Eleven: Consistency," I describe the consistency component for the building block of sustainability. The chapter defines ID Transformation as a journey rather than a destination. Creating a culture of ID Transformation is not a short-term goal to fix a problem but a long-term process to build a new environment. The consistency component builds a culture of belonging that requires patience. This chapter concludes with steps to follow when building a diversity program.

In "Chapter Twelve: Reflection," I discuss the reflection component for sustainability building block. The chapter explains the significance of creating a reflective environment that broadens worldviews that enhance organizational culture. A workplace environment that seeks transformation through critical thinking, creativity, and problem-solving will strengthen organizational capacity towards ID Transformation. This chapter ends with questions to ponder when building a diversity program.

Destination: ID Transformation

I suggest an additional building block to consider in Chapter Thirteen: Destination—ID Transformation, when creating an ID Transformational culture. I also describe how passion, authenticity, and knowledge are essential for achieving such a culture.

Conclusion and Epilogue

In my Conclusion, I discuss why workplace trust and respect are vital elements for leaders and staff if they are serious about implementing building blocks for their diversity program. I further review and emphasize the importance and consequence of organizational awareness, transformational leadership, and staff preparation in establishing an ID Transformational culture. Creating this type of culture is how any organization will be able to address cultural inequities and grow to its full potential.

Throughout the book, I develop the five building

blocks for implementing ID Transformational initiatives in institutions. In the Epilogue, I suggest an additional viewpoint for leaders to consider strengthening their commitment and sincerity as they utilize these building blocks. I also discuss insights on going beyond the rhetoric of diversity to discovering *a palpable sense of belonging that maximizes human and institutional capacity for progressive innovation.*

And now, without further ado, I present my building blocks for ID Transformation to you. The intent of my book is twofold: One is to provide a practical approach to developing a transformational diversity program that cuts through theory and rhetoric. Second, identify the missing components typically not addressed when starting a diversity program that is relevant and sustaining.

I reference personal challenges and empowering moments during my journey towards ID Transformation. My life journey has always embraced ID because it empowers relational interdependency that advances communities toward a higher quality of life. I hope something in this book will resonate within you to become a partaker in building a culture of ID Transformation that emanates from a heart of grace and a soul of love.

Dr. Vernon D. Franklin
Pittsburgh, Pennsylvania USA
October 2022

INTRODUCTION

"Everybody can be great because anybody can serve. You only
need a heart full of grace. A soul generated by love."
– Dr. Martin Luther King Jr.

This quote from Dr. King Jr. is the focus of my life
mission to develop a heart full of grace and a soul generated by love that empower others in teachable moments. My
mission to equip individuals through professional development has been my passion as a practitioner and educator while
serving in higher education communities for more than three
decades. Thus, my tenures at the University of Pittsburgh and
Community College of Allegheny County have provided me
an opportunity to serve while using my talents and skills to develop educational and professional efficacy in students, faculty,
and staff.

I am passionate about helping institutions achieve
their mission through inclusion and diversity initiatives. I am a
skilled professional trainer, instructor, and administrator, and a
lifelong learner who has dedicated my life-shaping experiences
to help individuals increase their educational and professional
potential. My life mission determines my practitioner blueprint
that has merged with my professional aim to develop practical
ways to achieve a productive workplace. Throughout my career, I designed and facilitated workshops and coursework in
diversity and inclusion, technology, leadership, and professional
development that continue to influence institutions. Hence, my
strategic planning, collaboration, team building, and professional development expertise all contributed to writing this book.

The need for this book arose from my inability to

discover information about developing a diversity program as a Diversity and Inclusion Program Manager. There is much discussion surrounding the theory and concepts of diversity and inclusion (DI) initiatives, but little on a systematic approach to develop such a program. Therefore, I created a practical model using five building blocks to guide the development of a diversity program for organizations.

My exposure to institutional issues surrounding diversity and inclusion have given me a passion for improving any culture that did not provide an equitable return to its staff. My life-shaping experiences are the lens through which I interpret a universe that reveals the omnipresence of diversity. Thus, my building blocks for ID Transformation are designed to help institutions lay the foundation that will build a workplace culture of connected individuals that produces a measurable sense of belonging, thus increasing human and organizational capacity for profitability—or whatever the bottom line is for the organization.

Exposure to diversity has been a significant life-shaping experience for me, resulting in personal, educational, and professional fulfillment. Having learned much through my journey, I embrace the value of diversity that has broadened my worldview. Beginning in elementary school, I was intrigued by classmates from different cultural backgrounds as we shared each other's customs and traditions. Those early life experiences prepared me for future educational, professional, and personal interactions and they continue to play an important role in my life journey. Being exposed to diversity has provided me with a lifetime of substantial relationships that have enhanced my understanding of social and cultural issues.

I have also witnessed social and cultural challenges when people with rigid biases are intolerant of others with different opinions. This lack of respect for other beliefs creates barriers to meaningful dialog and increased knowledge. Stephen Covey (1989) states, "First seek to understand, and then try to be understood." This principle has been a governing value that causes me to take the initiative to understand other viewpoints that often lead to synergy through our differences.

My life experiences have taught me that a competing opinion is not necessarily erroneous but should be critically examined with objectivity to gain a meaningful understanding that can then broaden my worldview.

My appreciation for social diversity has also taught me the importance of interdependency. In an interdependent culture, individuals are better listeners, supporters, and collaborators who then establish a more productive and creative environment. Diversity is a rich tapestry of social and cultural differences that can create significant interpersonal relationships resulting in individuals gaining new ways of thinking through collaboration.

Research suggests diversity programs in organizations increase creativity and productivity. Studies also indicate that many organizations face challenges when implementing diversity practices within the workplace. When organizations desire the benefits of diversity without investing the time to create a culture of belonging, they are "pouring new wine into old wineskins" as mentioned earlier, which results in nonproductive outcomes. Thus, an effective strategic plan unique to every organization must be developed, implemented, and continuously evaluated with empathy for all people groups if organizations wish to ensure ID Transformational practices are an integral part of their mission and values.

Within the last decade, the study of best practices for diversity has become popular in organizations. After leaders and staff receive information from conferences, workshops, and seminars, I wonder how they transfer what they have learned into the workplace. I wonder because many institutions have not established significant diversity programs capable of maximizing workplace outcomes conducive to either efficiency or innovation after all their studies.

Many organizations' motivation to adopt a diversity program stems from their expectations of their Return on Investments (ROI). Research has revealed that a diverse-and-inclusive-workplace culture enhances new ways of thinking, collaboration, and productivity that can contribute to an organization's bottom line. This book will guide leaders to go beyond the theoretical rhetoric of ROI when it comes to diversity. This will then help organizations take practical steps to build a culture of ID Transformation that is relevant, sustainable, and leads to a more robust bottom line.

During my initial years doing diversity work, it became apparent that managers hindered many progressive efforts in establishing a new culture. I experienced the blind-and-deaf syndrome of feeling unseen and unheard when presenting diversity proposals. Throughout my higher education tenure, most of my workplace proposals to management were not accepted for one reason or another, only to see them implemented as someone else's ideas.

When I received my doctorate in higher education management, the chief information officer (CIO), approached me to become the Diversity and Inclusion Program Manager for our department of more than three hundred staff. This was the third time in three decades that top leadership had *acknowledged my existence*, while I remained unseen by many middle managers during that tenure. No one had ever championed my cause that led to advancement. After several days of thinking about the new position offered, I accepted it because I understood the department's culture from my practitioner experience. I had developed and taught numerous technology and professional development courses, so this new role seemed like a good fit.

My first steps in my new position were to research what other institutions were doing in their diversity programs and also to set up an inclusion team to work with me. Shortly after I formed the inclusion team, the CIO retired, making diversity efforts more challenging under the new management, who indicated by their actions that they were not committed to diversity efforts.

I continued to work closely with the inclusion team, researched diversity best practices and challenges, participated in webinars, and attended conferences. It was exciting to participate in conferences on diversity because I received enlightening information and favorable feedback regarding my ideas on ID Transformation. Attending my initial diversity conference was the first time I felt like I was among peers dedicated to institutional inclusion that went beyond the rhetoric. I felt energized by the motivational discussions about institutional diversity. I longed for that same type of synergy at my workplace, where I had often felt like a prophet without honor in his own hometown when presenting my ideas.

Throughout my tenure in higher education, I have had many life-shaping experiences that broadened and shaped my worldview towards diversity. My environmental influences have shaped my worldview and prepared me to contribute to the discussion surrounding the development of institutional diversity programs. I designed the building blocks to include concepts I believe necessary for creating *a culture of relationally-interconnected individuals who create a palpable sense of belonging that increases human and organizational capacity for progressive innovation.* The purpose of my building blocks is to assist you in becoming more mindful of their effect on ID Transformation by being proactive towards influencing mindset growth in their organizations.

I desire that you begin to reflect upon your understanding and influences towards ID Transformation that has impacted your life for creating a community of belonging. Therefore, before we move on, take a look at this critical-thinking exercise which will be a regular part of this book going forward.

CRITICAL-THINKING EXERCISE

"The highest form of human excellence is to question oneself and others." —Socrates

If you desire to affect your world or organization, you must first practice self-reflection relative to your own life-shaping experiences that have contributed to your perspective towards diversity practices. Your worldview is the lens through which you interpret, engage in, and attempt to influence corporate culture where diversity is concerned. That's why it's important for you to be aware of what it is. That is the reason I recommend you begin and maintain a journal throughout your engagement with this book's material—so you can be aware.

An Example Of My Journaling

The first exercise in this book is to take time to journal life situations and experiences that have influenced your ideology towards DEI. Reflective journaling is a way to understand how social and cultural engagements have shaped your diversity ideology. Before writing a reflective journal, think about how your life-shaping experiences have created the lens through which you view diversity. Your environmental influences are from family, friends, school, and work. Think about how each environment influenced your ideology on cultural diversity. Was there exposure to different people groups? Can you explain positive and negative experiences regarding orientation or non-exposure to other people groups? Also, think about how your environment has created barriers or advantages for growth. To provide the context for your reflective journal, see Table 1 beginning on the following page.

TABLE 1: AUTHOR'S REFLECTIVE JOURNAL

RICH TAPESTRY OF DIVERSITY
"We all should know that diversity makes for a rich tapestry, and we must understand that all the threads of the tapestry are equal in value no matter what their color."
—Maya Angelou

DIVERSITY STATEMENT
Diversity has played a significant role in my life-shaping experiences, and I have always appreciated the experiences that broaden my worldview. Social diversity has taught me the importance of interdependency and has enhanced my interpersonal skills. Hence, I'm a better listener, supporter, and collaborator while I strive for consensus. Stephen Covey (2006) states that I must first seek to understand others and then try to be understood. This principle has been a transforming principle helping me understand and embrace cultural diversity. My life experiences have given me an appreciation for the rich cultural tapestry of diversity.

THE UNRAVELED TAPESTRY THREADS
I grew up in a lower middle-class home where family, community, and church were very supportive during my formative years, teaching me the value of meaningful relationships through different people groups. My years of attending elementary school were also influential in shaping my understanding and appreciation of cultural diversity. During my high school and undergrad college years, racism I experienced and witnessed changed my worldview, unraveling threads from my ideological tapestry of diversity. My introduction to racism's divisiveness was not limited to high school and college but continued throughout my professional career.
As a black male, the most significant unraveling for me occurred in higher learning institutions and the workplace.

While predominately white institutions challenged my ideology regarding an inclusive culture, I also had many encouraging experiences that prevented my tapestry of diversity from unraveling altogether. Both the negative and positive experiences shaped my worldview towards societal diversity and inclusion. The following are a few challenging life-shaping experiences:

- A secondary school counselor recommended that I no longer pursue an academic diploma designed to prepare students for college. Although I had a 3.4 grade point average, the counselor advised me to switch to the general diploma courses and enroll in a trades program. My parents and older sibling did not consent to the counselor's recommendation and made sure I remained in the academic program. Family members experienced many other discriminatory actions throughout their lives, and therefore knew the challenges ahead for me as a black male in America. They provided constructive encouragement, counsel, and guidance.

- Racial microaggressions were not isolated to secondary school but followed me throughout college. During my first year of college, an instructor recommended I drop out of college and go to a trade school when I had trouble with some coursework. This experience was one of the numerous faculty infractions and racial microaggressions that seemed never-ending.

- When entering the workplace of predominately white males, I felt invisible. It always seemed my white colleagues who had less educational background benefited from favoritism and advancements. Often, I provided new ideas which seemingly went unnoticed only to have them resurface later as new initiatives from white colleagues.

MENDING THE UNRAVELED THREADS

A system of cultural racism and inequality threatened to unravel my tapestry. However, despite the negative encounters, the positive family nurturers, supportive friendships, and the positive investment of other educators, counselors, and colleagues strengthened my rich tapestry of diversity that shaped my interactions and influence toward others.

PRESERVING THE TAPESTRY FROM RACISM

As a result of the historical underpinning of racism in our culture, racial inequities will be a part of America's social practices. Therefore, I join with other blacks, people of color, and whites committed to social justice that will preserve the rich tapestry of diversity from racism and microaggressions that weaken the threads in the tapestry.

LESSONS LEARNED THAT GUIDE MY INFLUENCE

I will always remember the advice of my parents as an adolescent: "There's no one better than you, and there's no one that you are better than." Because of family nurturing and people committed to social justice, I have survived cultural practices of inequities. Thus, I am committed to strengthening the threads in my diversity tapestry that contributes to building an inclusive culture embracing and promoting diversity within my influence.

DIVERSITY REFLECTIVE JOURNAL

After you read my reflective journal above, take time to reflect on your own experiences (positive and negative situations) that have influenced your worldview towards diversity. It doesn't have to be as well-developed or comprehensive as mine and you can continue to add to it as you read through the book. Knowing how you define a diversity ideology will determine your constructive or destructive capability of contributing toward ID Transformation. When writing your journal, be creative. It may help to find a quote or create your own quote on the topic of diversity or social justice that will guide your journaling.

1. Did you learn anything about yourself from journaling? If so, what are the encouraging and negative lessons learned that provided new insights?

2. In what ways can you build upon the encouraging insights and develop positive outcomes from undesirable life-shaping experiences?

3. How will lessons learned from your reflective journal influence your interpersonal communications toward ID Transformation?

Note: This exercise can also be used in your organization to help your staff write a personal diversity statement that will shape their attitude and commitment towards creating a workplace of belonging.

PART ONE

THE FOUNDATION FOR ID TRANSFORMATION

The phenomenon of technological advancement continues to create paradigm shifts within every area of society. Institutions must be equipped with the tools to successfully function while also transforming their staff to meet the needs and challenges of a progressive global community. Political, economic, social, and technology trends are reshaping today's workplace, thus creating an increased demand for adaptive leadership to navigate their organizations through the maze of change. In this Part One, you will read two chapters:

Chapter One: The Adaptive Challenge

Chapter Two: Vision

CHAPTER 1

THE
ADAPTIVE CHALLENGE

"The secret of change is to focus all your energy not on fighting the old but building the new." – Socrates

My building blocks will help organizations understand and create a culture that fosters and promotes ID Transformation. This culture depicts a *relational-interconnection among individuals that causes a palpable sense of belonging, thus increasing human and organizational capacity.* The five building blocks are a framework to guide organizations so they can devise principles for their diversity programs. However, their framework alone cannot sustain itself without a solid foundation. Thus, my building blocks for ID Transformation must rest on the foundation and be held together with the mortar of adaptive leadership and vision.

Before starting a diversity program, organizations must address diversity as an adaptive rather than only a technical challenge. The lack of adaptive leadership is one of several reasons for the disparity found in diversity programs. Thus, the following explains the concept of technical and adaptive challenges.

- A *technical* challenge responds to external problems by requiring the learning of new techniques or skills to increase competency. An example of this was when faculty, students, and staff would attend one of my productivity software workshops to improve their proficiency in using System Software or Office 365, thus helping them perform tasks to meet a workplace or classroom challenge.

- An *adaptive* challenge is how an individual responds to an environmental problem that requires a mindset or heart change, such as a soft skill that necessitates self-development. An example of this type of challenge and response is when I created a workshop to help staff examine themselves so they could discover ideologies that needed changing to effectively solve workplace diversity challenges. This workshop did not include the usual diversity training on biases but was a self-assessment session titled "Progressive Reframing Towards Diversity and Inclusion." The workshop model is outlined in chapter six.

It is important to make this distinction because not all challenges within organizations are the same. Organizational leaders must know the difference between an adaptive and technical challenge so they can respond appropriately and obtain a successful resolution.

Many organizations approach diversity programs as a technical problem and set out to fix diversity disparity, biases, and inequities because they see them as an external challenge. That may be the reason many diversity programs fail. Organizations will not solve diversity issues by learning new technical skills but rather by renewing and transforming the mindsets of the people involved. Instead, diversity is an *adaptive* problem that requires an inward mindset change to build a culture of ID Transformation. The bottom line for those who work in diversity programs is developing new ways of thinking. A diversity program *cannot* be successful without meeting the adaptive challenge by way of changed hearts and minds.

Not until I listened to a YouTube video with Dr. Joy DeGruy, keynote lecturer on the *Excellence Through Diversity Distinguished* at the UVA Engineering community, did I discover another vital concept for adaptive leaders. In that session, Dr. DeGruy pointed out that we cannot repair the barriers of organizational diversity if we can't see the barriers within ourselves or the organizational roots. My assessment for upholding the structure of ID Transformation is the foundation for such awareness. A solid foundation involves understanding and dismantling the grip of organizational obstacles rooted in inequities. Thus, *organizations can't heal what they don't see or understand.*

I once discussed the lack of diversity in our organization with one of my senior leaders. It was evident at our all-staff meetings that women and people of color were a minority of our 300-plus staff. The leader's response was that diversity wasn't an issue because diversity was in our organization's DNA. If leaders cannot recognize the disparity, then the efforts of a diversity program are futile.

The goal of a diversity program is to work towards converting diversity and inclusion from a recessive to a dominant gene in an organization's DNA. When diversity becomes the dominant gene, there will no longer be a need for diversity programs. But until then, organizations must be committed to achieving a seemingly impossible dream.

Ronald Heifetz (2009) suggests an adaptive challenge must invoke a different reaction beyond typical methods. Traditional problem-solving techniques will not produce a progressive diversity program that is relevant and sustainable because the dynamics of diversity are multifaceted. Thus, adaptive leadership ought to seek innovative ways to prepare staff for the changes needed to create a culture of ID Transformation.

Leaders should incorporate learning platforms that equip and empower organizational transformation. Leadership must also create an atmosphere of trust and respect within their organizations. Staff who trust and respect their leaders will be more willing to follow them, thus making it easier to commit to leadership's vision as they articulate and model the way for change.

To further understand the complexity of challenges, leaders must appropriately respond based on the different problem types. Author David Snowden (2022) provides more insight into why diversity programs fail in American organizations. He states that there are five decision-making domains:

simple, complicated, complex, chaotic, and disorder. Identifying what category a problem fits into helps leaders decide on an appropriate response. The following are examples of the type of problems mentioned:

- A simple problem relies on traditional methods for a solution that is an evident best practice.
- A complicated problem is when research and expertise outside the organization are needed to analyze the situation producing a good practice.
- A complex problem is a unique situation where collaboration and investigation are necessary for a solution that initiates an evolving practice.
- A chaotic problem is a disruptive condition that needs an immediate response to yield a novel practice.
- A disorder problem is when the problem type is not understood.

When leaders don't understand the type of problem diversity represents and how to respond appropriately, they cannot produce intended outcomes. In other words, they not only cannot solve the problem, but they may also make it worse. Many organizations do not realize that diversity is an adaptive challenge and approach it as a simple problem that can be addressed using traditional practices.

As a Diversity and Inclusion Program Manager, I viewed diversity in my institution as a combination of complicated and complex problems within the decision-making domains. Hence, my organization's inclusion team diligently researched good practices, sought outside expertise to develop good practices, and collaborated as a team to investigate organizational barriers and assets that initiated healing practices. When leaders approach diversity programs as an adaptive challenge and know what type of decision-making domain their organizations will face, it is an effective method that will produce meaningful and evolving practices within their organizations.

To meet the challenges of implementing a diversity program, adaptive leaders need to provide guidance amid seemingly constant paradigm shifts, which for many seem to be seismic in nature. Leaders' worldviews must constantly evolve to influence effective transformation among the staff. Kevin Cashman (2008) refers to this concept as leading from the inside out. Self-development and introspection are significant attributes for adaptive leaders who lead their teams through change. Joseph Rost (1993) stated that leadership must commit to transforming both their staff and organization.

Change is an arduous process for most people and many individuals struggle with it. Therefore, adaptive leadership should prepare to lead and assist staff in seeking new ways of collaborating to meet the demanding dynamics of a changing workplace. Despite individual and organizational challenges and fears in an era of COVID-19, technological advancements, social inequities, and political divide, adaptive leaders must create new opportunities for staff transformation despite the turmoil of social issues.

Socrates stated, "An unexamined life is not worth living." That provides a realistic observation for the importance of self-development. Thus, when more emphasis is placed on self-transformation, it will result in environmental change. Imagine the untapped productivity and innovation awaiting to emerge when institutions increase their commitment to inward change.

Albert Einstein is quoted as saying, "The day that humanity and technology overlap, humanity will become idiots." Here's a question I ask my information technology students: Is Albert Einstein's quote a prophetic insight regarding the overlap of humanity and technology referring to Biological Technology and Artificial Intelligence (AI)? I pose the same question to you.

Research suggests that 80% of society does not seek change. Another finding stated that 90% of the population think they are self-aware, but the study found only 10% to 15% are. When I think about these research studies and Einstein's prophecy, it explains why diversity programs in American institutions are not successful, as mentioned in the Maverick Findings (2019):

- Diversity training and programs are extremely popular and viewed positively by participants but have not delivered any notable improvement in workplace diversity.

- Awareness programs focused on changing biases are ineffective and tend to increase sensitivity to the biases of others without improving awareness of personal biases.

- Homogeneous teams are more confident and happier but perform poorly—in contrast to diverse teams that perform well, but do not feel as successful or effective.

There are numerous resources regarding organizational change that leaders have drawn from to develop their organizations. Many leaders have mastered the principles and tools for project management and training but have less expertise in human transformation. When organizations mirror societal fears, tribalism, biases, racism, and inequities, they create barriers that undermine ID Transformation. For a sense of belonging to thrive in organizations, leaders must dismantle the nonproductive ideologies that resist change within themselves and their organizations.

I suggest that historical underlying ideologies of inequities within organizational cultures hinder the development of an authentic ID Transformation. Whenever leaders and staff honestly seek inward growth and transformation, it will erode a synthetic form of ID Transformation. An organization energized by diverse and evolving mindsets will ignite an innovative workplace of *relationally-interconnected individuals causing a palpable sense of belonging that increases human and organizational capacity for progressive innovation.* From my professional observation, the five building blocks for ID Transformation need to be part of any organizational strategy if diversity programs are to create the intended results in organizations.

Hopefully, you learned in this chapter that organizational diversity leaders must know the difference between adaptive and technical challenges along with understanding decision-making domains. Depending on the problems within an organization, the right approach to solve a challenge is crucial for the intended outcomes. It is natural for leaders to solve a problem by defaulting to technical means, for issues that require an innovative solution require an inward change in perspective that isn't as obvious or intuitive. Human-caused issues perpetuated within organizations must be resolved by a change in behavioral practices. A technical approach can't remedy problems of inequities.

Intentional actions are required if we are serious about correcting diversity disparities caused by human behaviors. These actions are like solving an algebraic equation that must perform a negative and positive action on both sides to create a balance. Thus, the positive human interventions must reverse the negative barriers caused by human interactions (or inaction). Constructive human efforts toward advancing organizational diversity require an inward mindset change to meet the adaptive challenges that tend to resist ID Transformation.

CRITICAL-THINKING EXERCISE

For this critical-thinking exercise, do the following:

1. Refer to the following meanings of technical and adaptive challenges, and then think about situations when you responded to an adaptive challenge using a technical method.

    - A *technical* challenge responds to an external problem requiring learning new techniques or skills to increase competency.

    - An *adaptive* challenge is how an individual responds to an environmental problem that requires a mindset or heart change, such as a soft skill that requires self-development.

2. Think about situations in your diversity program and identify which are adaptive or technical challenges.

3. Think about how you would approach them based on identifying them as an adaptive and technical challenge.

4. Think about and list any nonproductive mindsets within your organization toward diversity that need to change.

5. What are the nonproductive attitudes that need to change in order to adapt to diversity challenges?

6. Think about how your organization can

collectively address and change any nonproductive mindsets towards diversity initiatives.

From your answers and responses to the six points above, sketch out a preliminary action plan that will help change your mindset, broaden your worldview, and influence your organization's diversity program.

CHAPTER 2

VISION

"It is the set of the sails, not the direction of the wind that determines which way we will go." – Jim Rohn

Before developing a diversity program, there must be a unified definition for diversity. As you learned in the previous chapter, an individual's interpretation of diversity comes from their life-shaping experiences, which means that organizations with people from various cultural backgrounds contain a potpourri of subjective diversity ideologies. My first step in developing a diversity program at my institution was to create a consensus regarding an ideal working experience that captures a unified practice. I came up with the word *belonging* and expanded upon its meaning to describe how a sense of belonging feels to an individual, and used words like connect, respect, contribute, and embrace.

My interpretation of belonging additionally changed the common reference for diversity and inclusion to the following: #Inclusion*Then*Diversity. This rebranding repositions the order of the wording, so the focus is no longer on fixing a problem but building a new culture of *ID Transformation where there are relationally-interconnected individuals that foster a palpable sense of belonging that increases both the human and organizational capacity for progressive innovation.* When I proposed the concept of belonging be part of my organization's diversity program, the suggestion was received unanimously by the department's CIO and inclusion team I had formed.

Instead of organizations focusing on biases training

(which has been proven nonproductive), they should instead concentrate on behavioral patterns that people can identify with and then use those to hold one another accountable. This approach is less threatening and creates a harmonious environment that fosters and promotes behavioral patterns that foster inclusivity. As society evolves at an extraordinary pace, the traditional diversity program must be transformative. If organizations are going to benefit from their perceived outcomes that diversity generates, then they will need to be critical thinkers and become creative in developing programs that are more progressive while producing tangible results.

Creating an organizational brand and charter for a diversity program creates a realistic vision to guide leaders and staff throughout their development and implementation process. The following are my two steps that create a cohesive understanding and buy-in for leaders and staff. First, a *brand* provides a unified definition, and second, a *charter* establishes goals and objectives for diversity practices that contribute toward developing a relevant and sustainable vision within an organization.

Organizational Branding

An example of branding is a logo or motto that represents a shared definition for diversity that embodies an acceptable and expected behavior pattern within a workplace culture. The branding must be stated in clear and understandable terminology that describes a vision for the organization. Figure 1 is an example of a branding model for a diversity program.

In Figure 1, I stressed for my organization that *belonging* achieves an inclusive culture that embraces diversity—which is the centerpiece. The interdependent components of *belonging* are connect, respect, contribute, and embrace. These components establish a culture of belonging among leadership and staff where they feel a sense of relationship that values their input from a different background and perspective. This environment results in new ways of thinking and increases productivity and innovation. Belonging, however, does not constitute assimilation or groupthink but advocates diverse uniqueness that works together toward a shared mission.

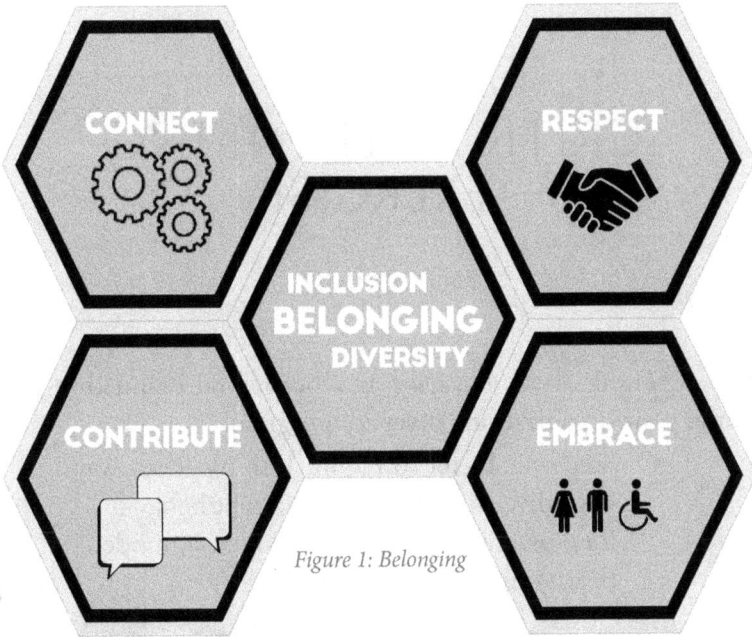

Figure 1: Belonging

Organizational Charter

An effective organizational charter goes beyond setting workplace policies and procedures. It must specify clear, concise, and short- and long-term directives that achieve significant outcomes aligned with the intended organizational diversity goals. (Please refer to "Appendix: Guide for Organizational Inclusion and Diversity (ID) Charter" as a guide to consider when drafting an organizational charter.)

The organizational brand and charter are at the core of the institution's mission and culture. All organization stakeholders have a unique, clearly-defined purpose in the brand and charter that enhances the institutional mission of belonging. Gary Kramer (2010) argues that senior leadership have an obligation to promote a collaborative culture toward a common goal. Thus, an overarching vision is a means to establish a culture of belonging through a well-designed brand and charter. A vision also provides a strategic guide for leaders and staff to develop a culture of ID Transformation that involves all stakeholders.

CRITICAL-THINKING EXERCISE

Think about *belonging* as a behavioral brand that will guide your organization's diversity program.

- Step one: Refer to Figure 1, think about ways your diversity program can adopt behavioral practices for staff to follow that model belonging.

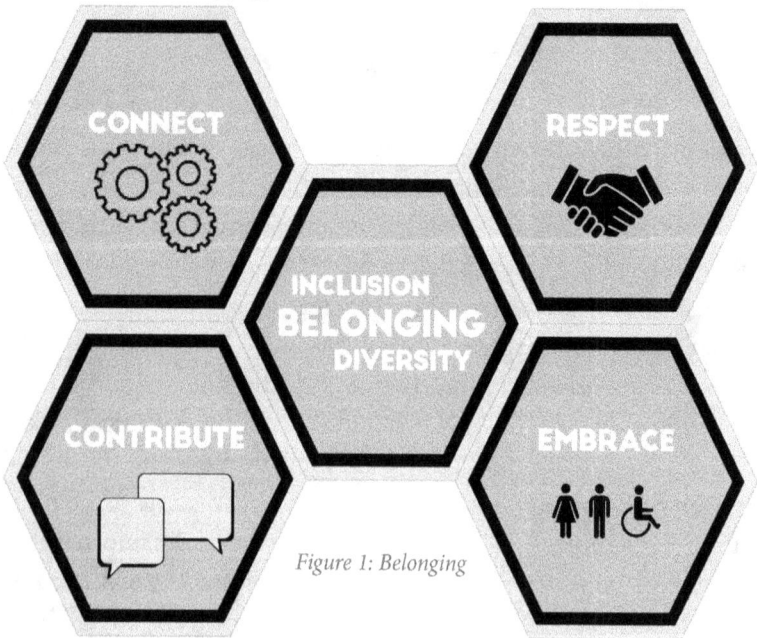

Figure 1: Belonging

- Step two: Take note of other organizations with diversity branding and compare them to a culture of belonging.
- Step three: Create a *belonging* brand for your

diversity program that will be a visual definition so everyone can understand the vision.

Note: My vision for belonging needed more clarity in determining what it meant, thus, referencing inclusion then diversity, in this order, while then providing four core behavioral practices (connect, respect, contribute, and embrace) that defined my idea of belonging, as seen in figure 1.

Charter

A charter defines the function of an organization; thus, the diversity program charter in this chapter illustrates agreed-upon commitments and goals. This exercise is for thinking about your diversity program's goals and accountability. The following steps will help guide and measure successful outcomes for your diversity program's goals.

- Step one: Think about two short-term and long-term goals for your diversity program.
- Step two: If you need goal ideas for your diversity program, refer to the goals examples under the action plan on the *Guide for Organizational Inclusion and Diversity (ID) Charter* located in the Appendix.
- Step three: Based on your listed goals, answer the following action plan metrics questions for each goal:

1. What resources are needed?

2. How are you going to be held responsible?

3. How are you going to measure your improvement?

4. By what date do you want to reach your goal?

5. How can you assess the results of your outcomes?

6. What are your key performance indicators (tangible objectives)?

This action plan question metric is a tool to help guide your diversity program's accountability process.

PART TWO

BUILDING BLOCKS FOR ID TRANSFORMATION

In Part Two, we will look at the five building blocks for ID Transformation that your organization can use when creating a diversity program. Each building block consists of two chapters describing a component that makes up the building block. Many diversity programs focus on correcting the diversity disparity by establishing new hiring practices along with bias training. While these are important initiatives, they do not address the big picture of creating a more inclusive culture.

Temporary fixes do not address a bridge's structural damage while its support beams crumble. The same is true when diversity programs are band-aid approaches to address historical inequalities within many organizations. Focusing on quick fixes and temporary solutions will impede the successful outcomes of ID Transformation. The five building blocks in this section are methods that strengthen and create a more inclusive organizational culture that embraces diversity.

The following outline for Part Two gives you an overview of the ID Transformational Building Blocks, each one containing two components:

Building Block One:
Organizational Awareness
Chapter Three: Culture
Chapter Four: Accountability

Building Block Two:
Transformational Leadership
Chapter Five: Influence
Chapter Six: Worldview

Building Block Three:
Staff Preparation
Chapter Seven: Purpose
Chapter Eight: Advancement

Building Block Four:
Empathetic planning
Chapter Nine: Strategy
Chapter Ten: Collaboration

Building Block Five: Sustainability
Chapter Eleven: Consistency
Chapter Twelve: Reflection

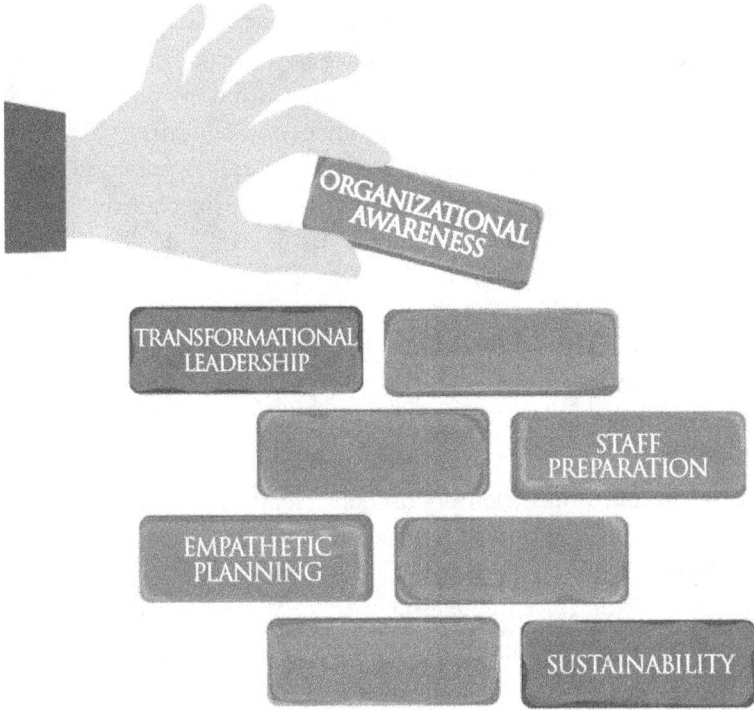

TRANSFORMATIONAL LEADERSHIP

ORGANIZATIONAL AWARENESS

STAFF PREPARATION

EMPATHETIC PLANNING

SUSTAINABILITY

CHAPTER 3

CULTURE

*"A people without the knowledge of their past history,
origin and culture is like a tree without roots."*
– Marcus Garvey

At the 2018 Human Capital Institute Conference, Dr. David Rock, CEO of the NeuroLeadership Institute, was a keynote speaker and provided insight into institutional diversity initiatives throughout America. Dr. Rock made a profound statement based on research results compiled by his Institute.

It gave me pause when he stated that diversity programs in many organizations in the U.S. would receive a failing grade, and companies that think they are successful would receive a D grade. Dr. Rock's research results were surprising and disappointing, given the number of seminars and workshops that are currently focusing on the best practices and benefits of diversity.

After recovering from my initial shock, I reflected upon the work surrounding diversity within the institution where I was serving to uncover evidence of failure. I decided to use Edgar Schein's organizational culture definition as my tool for evaluation. Schein (1998) stated that there are three components to examine when trying to understand an entity's culture: artifacts, espoused values, and underlying assumptions.

- *Artifacts* are the physical layout of the organization and can serve to define and reveal its cultural makeup. For example, individual office space and high cubicles can imply a culture that embraces privacy; open and shared areas can indicate an engaging and collaborative culture.

- *Espoused values* are tangible things written and spoken, such as mission and value statements, and slogans. Espoused values are expectations that establish behavior patterns within an organizational culture, helping to clarify purpose and shape daily interactions. When drafting espoused values, leaders and staff cultivate them as a planter does with a seed. A planter does not plant a seed without nurturing its growth. The same is true for leaders and staff who after drafting a mission and values (seeds) must cultivate the espoused values by articulating and modeling them to foster buy-in. Translating espoused values into action is essential when establishing or changing a culture.

- *Underlying assumptions* are the actual behavioral patterns of leaders and staff, and include how individuals conduct business practices, collaborate with colleagues, and interact with customers.

These sometimes unconscious behavioral patterns can be in or out of alignment with the espoused values. Espoused values must reflect the organization's culture through the underlying assumption—actual behaviors of how individuals perform duties and treat others, whether conscious or unconscious.

Schein (1998) provided an interesting lily-pond metaphor to define his three-levels of culture:

The blossoms and the leaves on the surface of the pond are the "artifacts" that we can see and evaluate. The farmer who has created the pond (the leadership) announces what he expected and hoped for in the way of leaves and blooms and will provide publicly accepted beliefs and values to justify the outcome. The farmer may or may not be consciously aware that the outcome is really a result of how the seeds, that root system, the quality of the water in the pond, and fertilizers he put in combined to create the blossoms and leaves. This lack of awareness of what actually produces the results may not matter if the announced beliefs and values are congruent with how the leaves and blooms turned out (p. 25).

When I consider Schein's culture model and my experiences with diversity work, I conclude there is substantial evidence of a disconnect between espoused values and underlying assumptions within cultural behavior patterns. Many institutions provide educational platforms that offer diversity training yet still fail to establish a culture of belonging as suggested by the NeuroLeadership Institute research. Since staff interactions within an organization emanate from their organization's cultural roots their underlying assumptions are the real seeds planted and then nurtured through staff and public interactions—not what an organization says is true but what is true based on day-in, day-out realities.

Dr. Rock's findings were predictable because there is such a wide disconnect between organizational espoused values and underlying assumptions. In other words, we tend to say one thing and do (or be) another. When organizations implement diversity initiatives with a bottom-up approach (staff then leaders), there are negative outcomes because leaders are not leading the way. If diversity efforts are not at the core of an organization's culture, workplaces will never earn higher than a D grade on the NeuroLeadership grading scale.

My culture component is a significate part of the organizational awareness building block. Before implementing a diversity program, time must be given to understanding the organizational culture through evaluation and assessment measurement tools. A strategy that does not consider an understanding of the organizational strengths, weaknesses, opportunities, and threats associated with diversity is flawed. The first step towards taking into consideration a program is understanding the current culture and efforts that must be involved in creating an ideal culture of belonging.

Schein provides a practical illustration of culture, but you may be wondering how it relates to diversity, equity, and inclusion (DEI). Therefore, I will further explain culture and its relevance. The culture component for the building block of organizational awareness is a way of life expressed through norms and practices. People adopt behavioral practices, beliefs, and values within this system without consciously thinking about them. Thus, different ethnic groups embrace their unique cultural norms and practices throughout generations.

Think about some of the cultural practices that define you as part of an ethnic group. Many of the norms have become rooted in your way of life. Whatever people group you identify with, consider how your practices relate to Schein's definition of cultural archives, espoused values, and underlying assumptions. You may also find disconnects within your culture's mottos, values, and practices.

As you think about the possible disconnects within your ethnic culture, focus on Schein's organizational culture from a broader perspective. Imagine the complexity of your cultural practices interwoven within an organization's culture of numerous ethnicities. It can be overwhelming to create an organization's culture from various cultural espoused values that are disconnected from how individuals interact daily (underlying assumptions).

The relevance of cultural diversity merging into one organization (melting pot) can be pretty challenging. It can present a monumental task of bringing together a potpourri of mindsets from different backgrounds into a harmonious cultural sense of belonging fueled by interdependency. Diversity does not constitute genetic interactions that generate inclusion. Where there is an assortment of cultural norms, inclusion can become messy and uncomfortable.

Within an organization of numerous cultures, leaders and staff can be inflexible in negotiating new cultural norms and values for the organization's good. In most cases, from previous generations the dominant culture within an organization established cultural norms. The perpetuation of many organizational norms has been maintained and continued without checking for disconnects in values and practices. Thus, the current culture can be out of sync with its espoused values and underlying assumptions. Still, the dysfunctionality continues to be in conflict with existing staff and new hires' competing cultural practices. Another misconception about inclusion within many organizations is that when staff adopt the cultural status quo, it is labeled inclusive. However, that's not inclusion, it's assimilation.

Creating new organizational cultural practices can be a challenge because of cultural disconnects and resistance toward new norms and values within organizations. Therefore, periodic reviews of the organizational missions and values are necessary. This re-examination process involves reassessing the vision to ensure that espoused values and underlying assumptions are aligned. The following chapter discusses an accountability component that will also guide cultural reassessment. Transformational leaders and staff passionate about what diversity can bring to organizational advancement must be the ones to lead this effort. These diversity workers are also committed to working through uncomfortable situations associated with inclusion to discover golden nuggets for creating an ID Transformational culture.

The implementation of a diversity program is an adaptive challenge that Ronald Heifetz (2009) claims will only succeed with new learning and knowledge outside of usual methods. In other words, it's going to require change and Schein stated that this change is long term and can take five or even ten years. There are no shortcuts. Thus, resources must be available to support the ongoing adaptive challenges while understanding and developing a new cultural environment.

When leaders do not understand their organization's cultural makeup and do not prepare staff for change before implementing initiatives, it leads to non-productive outcomes that actually work against the stated goal of diversity and inclusion. Also, in many organizations, diversity programs present new norms of practices. Thus, old implementation methods cannot sustain a new system of order. It is once again tantamount to the ancient warning not to pour new wine into old wineskins as stated in the preface. Consequently, leaders are responsible for creating a sustainable learning culture that can adapt to change.

There have been significant efforts made to hire diversity coordinators who can implement programs and training. Ironically, many institutions champion staff who can respond to customer needs and will find many ways to train them to be more effective. Yet somehow the same organizations can't seem to respond to the challenges toward creating an inclusive culture from the complexity of diversity. So, why don't leaders take initiative to comprehend the historical and current influences (good and bad) to develop an ID Transformational culture of *relationally-interconnected individuals who create a palpable sense of belonging that increases human and organizational capacity for progressive innovation?* Perhaps it is because they are not aware of the value—or aren't prepared to pay the price for change.

As stated earlier, Joseph Rost (1993) states that leadership must commit to the transformation of their organization's culture. Change is an arduous process for most people, and it is no secret that many individuals struggle with it. Adaptive change must begin with the leaders, but they can only lead as far as they have grown personally and professionally.

CRITICAL-THINKING EXERCISE

Let's review once again Schein's three levels of organizational culture:

- *Artifacts* are the physical layout of the organization and can serve to define and reveal its cultural makeup.
- *Espoused values* are tangible things written and spoken, such as mission and value statements, and slogans.
- *Underlying assumptions* are the actual behavioral patterns of leaders and staff, and include how individuals conduct business practices, collaborate with colleagues, and interact with customers.

Now think about the following questions:

1. What are your organization's artifacts, espoused values, and underlying assumptions?
2. Within your organization, is each level of culture in alignment? If so, explain how they support and advance your organizational purpose.
3. Are there any levels of your culture that are disconnected? If so, what are they?
4. If the disconnect is between the espoused values and underlying assumptions, consider what processes need to be implemented to bring them into alignment.

Now think about how well your personal values and actions align with your organization's values and actions.

1. How can you influence your organization to go

beyond the failures toward successful outcomes?

2. What are the needs in your organization's diversity program that may not be evident to others, but they are to you?

3. In what ways can diversity, equity, and inclusion be ingrained into your organizational culture?

When institutions are developing or strengthening their diversity programs, they should consider the above questions. Leaders and staff must also be creative in building a relevant foundation of norms that will support a sustainable culture of belonging that will become a part of their entity's DNA. In thinking about the questions, I posed, how can you collaborate with colleagues to go beyond what has been done or discussed to build a diversity program that creates a culture of ID Transformation, which is both relevant and sustainable in the twenty-first century?

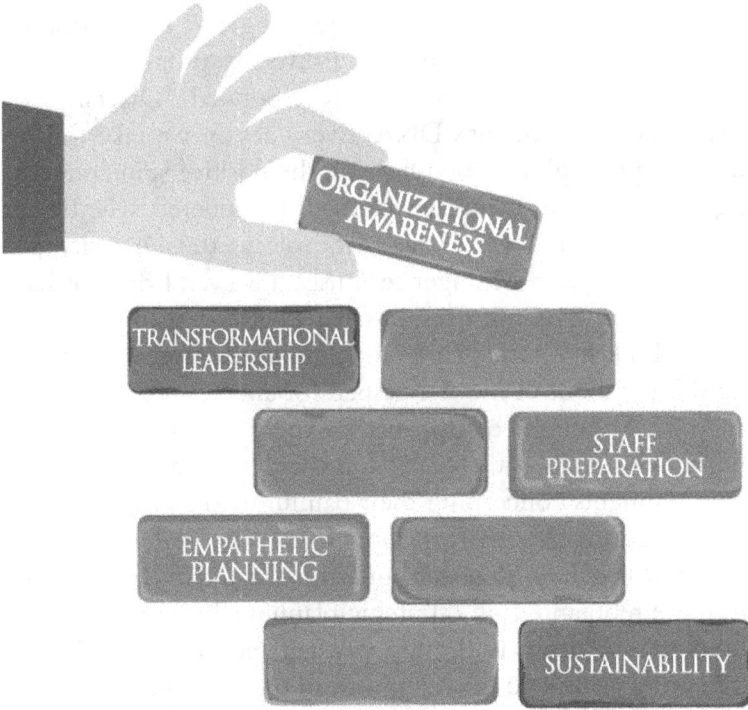

TRANSFORMATIONAL LEADERSHIP

ORGANIZATIONAL AWARENESS

STAFF PREPARATION

EMPATHETIC PLANNING

SUSTAINABILITY

CHAPTER 4

ACCOUNTABILITY

*"It is not only what we do, but also what we do not do,
for which we are accountable."* – Moliere

My Practitioner's Lens

As a Diversity and Inclusion Program Manager, I was
excited about the opportunity to intentionally build a more
inclusive workplace culture along with a strategic plan for reorganization. I was glad that diversity rhetoric would finally be

put into action. That was a breath of fresh air, but it didn't last long.

During a staff meeting regarding the reorganization strategic plan, I questioned why a diversity proposal wasn't a part of the plan. Senior leadership responded, "Diversity is a part of our department's DNA. Every action we take follows inclusive principles." When hearing the positive spin concerning our diversity workplace climate, I pondered whether to remain silent. If I was to take my role as the Diversity and Inclusion Program Manager seriously, however, I did not have the option of avoiding a response to what had been said.

I felt like someone had hit me in my stomach, knocking the wind out of me as I gasped for air. As I considered my response, I thought of the many experiences of feeling like the invisible man at the table along with hearing confidential staff comments concerning their painful workplace exclusions and infractions. Also, it was ironic that I was the Diversity and Inclusion Program Manager but felt isolated and disconnected from the reorganization's strategic planning. I will never forget those remarks from leadership or their rationale for omitting diversity policies and procedures from the strategic plan.

As a black male, I had learned the necessary survival techniques when working in an institution where many of my ideas seemed not to be accepted. Containing my disappointment, I calmly responded that diversity DNA most definitely should be a part of our culture but at the moment it was only an espoused organizational vision. My purpose for establishing an inclusion team was to adopt and enact policies and procedures for best practices to ensure that one day diversity and belonging would become part of our DNA. I informed leadership that as of that moment, we had not arrived as they thought. We had only begun to build a foundation to achieve a culture of inclusion that embraced diversity.

My statement did not receive any resistance, but I felt my comments fell on deaf ears. The leadership's perspective was subjective and not based on metrics from Climate and Workplace Experience Surveys, the results of which had never been implemented. My component for accountability described in this chapter provides the means by which any organization can assess whether or not there is evidence of diversity within the cultural DNA of their organization.

Accountability Component

Many organizations face challenges creating inclusive cultures that embrace diversity because they have an ideology of inequity. For organizations to obtain increased productivity and job proficiency that diverse mindsets bring to the workplace, leaders and staff must understand the benefits of embracing different mindsets. To ensure positive results, organizations can develop policies and procedures that support and monitor ID Transformational initiatives.

Higher education institutions have accreditation standards that hold them accountable for student learning outcomes. The same assessment standards would prove beneficial in keeping organizations responsible for ID Transformational outcomes. Leaders and staff play significant roles in supporting a shared vision that drives an accountability process to provide evidence of a culture of ID transformation.

Figure 2 illustrates standard practices for examining success or failure outcomes for an ID Transformational culture.

Accountability is the last step in the circular processes that validates the cultural intent. Although accountability appears to conclude the process, it is actually the continuous initiation of the checks and balances that does so. Accountability requirements comprise a system responsible for assessing performance conditions. Thus, accountability establishes a course of action needed. It either maintain benchmark successes or develop a different trajectory for failed outcomes. The successful or failed outcomes are determined from the strategic plan, evaluation, improvement, and assessment to achieve the intended Key Performance Indicators (KPI) for a culture of ID Transformation.

Accountability Process

The following are interdependent elements for the accountability component that produce positive cultural outcomes while establishing clear evidence of ID Transformation in an organization:

1. *Mission* sets the visionary directives by establishing outcomes that produce evidence of an inclusive culture while embracing diversity in its practices. Leadership must articulate the organization's mission that stimulates staff partnership in creating continual evaluation, improvement, and assessment for quality assurance and effectiveness.

2. *Strategic planning* establishes a shared partnership approach in which leaders and staff work together to develop policies and procedures for a diversity program. An effective strategic plan must also be aligned with the institutional mission that provides clarity and quality assurance for establishing a sense of belonging.

3. *Evaluation* guidelines are established to measure the culture's status which also help to determine action steps for improvement. Gary Kramer (2010) states the evaluation process provides clarity, and the necessary steps that result in institutional effectiveness as related to assessment standards. A starting point for leaders and staff is articulating and drafting the strengths, weaknesses, opportunities, and threats associated with an ideal culture that is both inclusive and diverse.

4. *Improvement* guidelines correlate with the results from the evaluation analysis and provide evidence of organizational strengths, weaknesses, opportunities, and threats that lead to an action plan to improve the culture. The improvement plan must also include a learning-and-development program that supports a significant move towards the intended ideal culture of ID Transformation.

5. *Assessment* guidelines are important to determine the successes and failures of the improvement action plan. The organization must determine KPI, such as a sense of belonging within the culture. A KPI is a benchmark that will determine a successful or unsuccessful outcome.

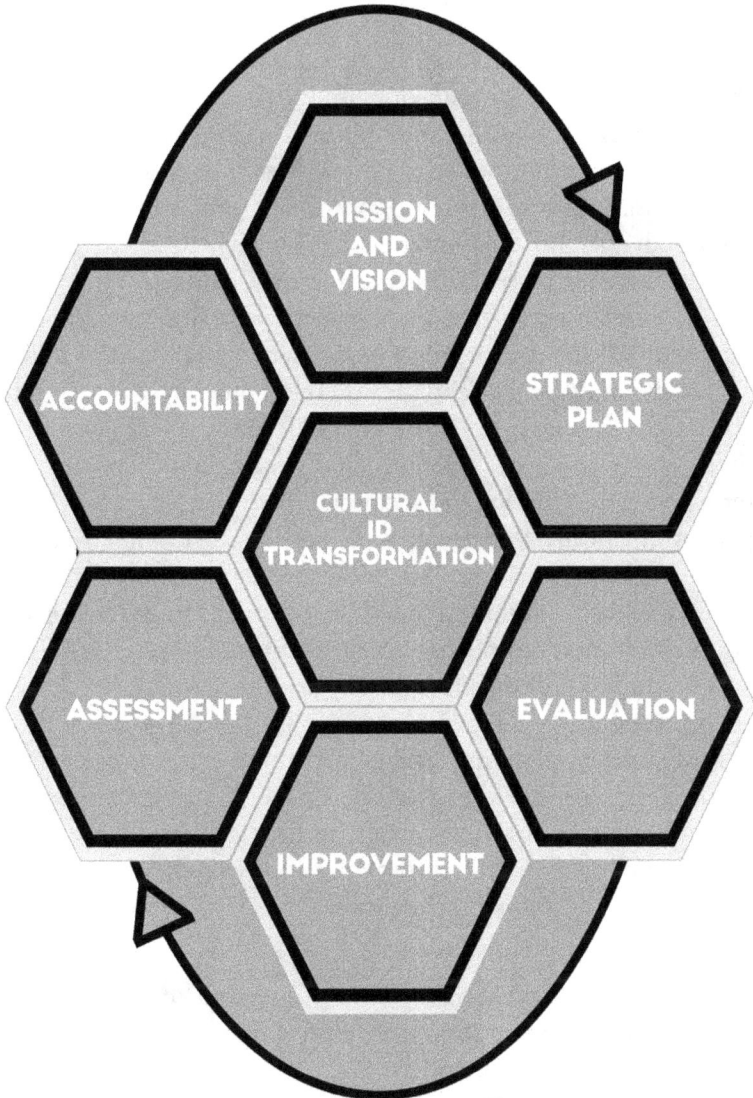

Figure 2: Accountability

The accountability component for building block one is the last process on the circular diagram that determines whether ID Transformational outcomes are successful or not. The circular diagram flow begins with mission, vision, and strategic planning for establishing a culture of ID Transformation that is part of the alignment and measurement process for accountability.

Accomplishment Through Quality Assurance

All leaders and staff work within the framework of a shared vision to impact accountability for ID Transformation. To affect the core outcomes for belonging, assertive efforts within an organization must be constantly measured through evaluation, improvement, and assessment initiatives. Thus, the intended goal for accountability is to provide evidence for achieved goals for an ID Transformational culture.

Implementing systematic review and adjustment of practices must also be part of the strategic planning for accountability. When the strategic plan and measurement processes for accountability function independently or inefficiently, it will jeopardize the diversity program's relevance and sustainability. Creating interdependencies among the accountability processes do not happen automatically; leaders and staff must be the driving agents.

Scholarly evidence supports the need for leaders to cultivate a culture committed to a shared purpose in providing accountability that connects with an institutional mission. Thus, accountability will establish quality assurance standards for diversity programs. Michael Middaugh (2011) suggests the process of strategic planning, evaluation, improvement, and assessment leads to institutional effectiveness. There are numerous measurement tools and resources for evaluation, improvement, and assessment from which organizations can choose to guide their specific accountability practices.

Synergistic Effort

The following are ways leadership can influence and inspire an institution-wide commitment to establish ID Transformation accountability:

1. Articulate a shared institutional mission and vision for cultural belonging. Leadership needs to say it as often as possible through various means.
2. Instill a value of continuous learning and development.
3. Establish avenues of communication to address and solicit feedback regarding evaluation, improvement, and assessment standards.

A well-functioning institution examines its effectiveness by incorporating guidelines that ensure accountability. Leaders and staff working together contribute synergistic efforts that constantly evaluate, improve, and assess outcomes according to pre-determined accountability standards for a culture of ID Transformation benchmarks.

The accountability component for building block one provides criteria for measuring the evidence in achieving a culture of ID Transformation that increases human and organizational capacity. The evidence of belonging in an organization is an intended key performance indicator. Diversity workers must understand the current makeup of their organization's culture and what they desire to achieve through their established initiatives. My accountability component for building block one is an approach to sustain a culture of ID Transformation through planning, evaluation, and improvement efforts.

CRITICAL-THINKING EXERCISE

Think about how you would develop your organization's accountability process for cultural ID Transformation:

- Step one: Think about your organization's diversity vision.
- Step two: Reflect on how your organization will achieve its vision for diversity.
- Step three: Refer to Figure 2, think about how it relates to your organization's accountability mechanism for a diversity program.
- Step four: Think about how evaluation, improvement, and assessment methods will help achieve your organization's diversity vision.
- Step five: Follow my accountability process cycle and create an accountability process for your organization that will sustain a culture of ID Transformation.
- Step six: Do research on evaluation, improvement, and assessment measurement tools that your organization can use for accountability guidelines.

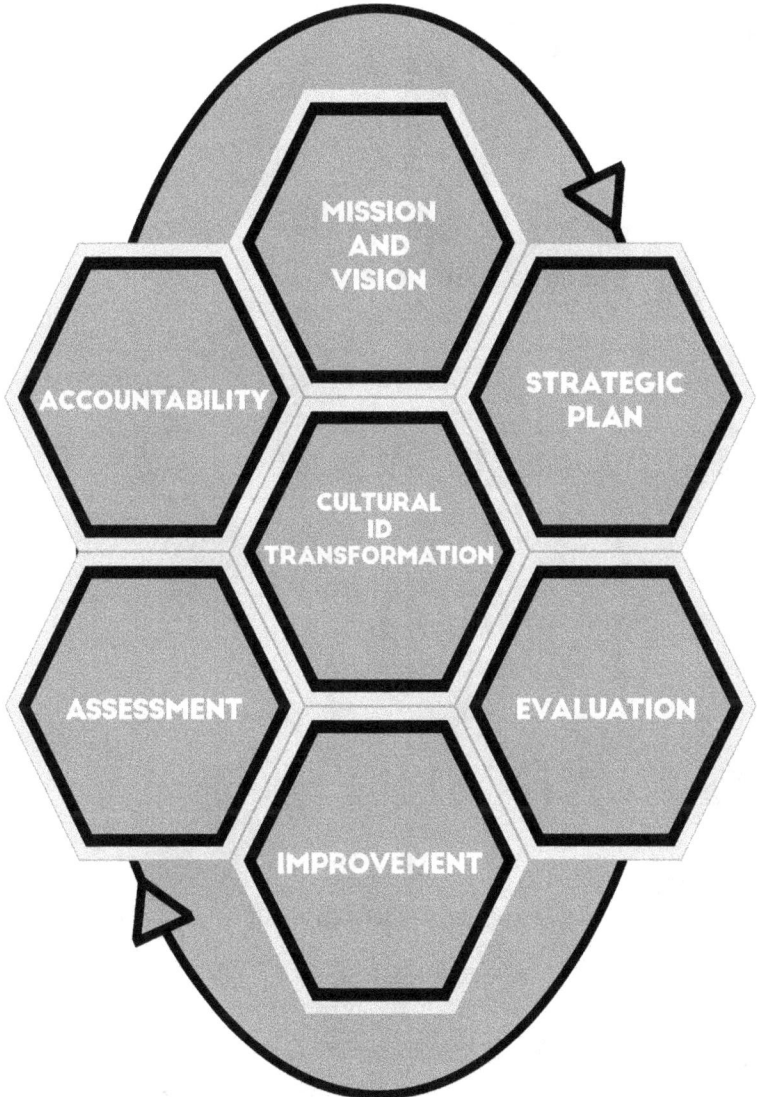

Figure 2: Accountability

TRANSFORMATIONAL
LEADERSHIP

ORGANIZATIONAL
AWARENESS

STAFF
PREPARATION

EMPATHETIC
PLANNING

SUSTAINABILITY

CHAPTER 5

INFLUENCE

"The key to successful leadership today is influence, not authority." – Ken Blanchard

My Practitioner's Lens

The content for this book emerged from my workplace experiences that created barriers preventing me and others from achieving our fullest potential. At times, I felt trapped behind a brick wall of isolation, struggling to find support to grow and thrive. There was a lack of managerial interest in my career development while I witnessed other colleagues advancing in theirs. This experience created a doubt that I was good enough to merit their attention or effort for advancement. Although I was competent, years of feeling neglected and invisible came from workplace managers who could not (or would not) motivate or direct my development.

Despite my academic achievements and job qualifications, it seemed most superiors never encouraged me to reach beyond my potential. I also never felt a sense of belonging throughout most of my professional career even though I received affirmation from family, community, church, and volunteer agencies outside the workplace. Despite those perceived obstacles within the work environment, there were seeds of encouragement from outside supporters. These encouragers were sources of influence that allowed me to see the potential that workplace managers could not provide.

If you feel under-appreciated and devalued in your organization, I encourage you to find your fertile ground. You can grow despite an indifferent or even hostile workplace situation. Recognizing your significance and motivating yourself to show up every day, do your best, and be your authentic self are the first steps in discovering your hidden talents, passion, and life purpose.

Many managers I worked with throughout my career were not malicious but could not see my potential or help nurture it because of three life-shaping factors: a narrow worldview, blind-spots, and a lack of transformational skills. Managers see through the lens of their own life-shaping experiences. Not having an accurate understanding of different groups or how they (the managers) are perceived can distort how they see potential—in themselves or in others. Also, when individuals are not committed to personal transformation and lifelong learning, their capacity to be transformative and influential is limited. I often wondered how much farther I would have advanced and how much I would have accomplished if a transformational manager had seen my potential.

Influence Component

Butterflies are beautiful and fascinating phenomenon of nature. A butterfly is not born as butterfly—it goes through metamorphosis. There are four stages—egg, caterpillar, chrysalis, and butterfly—through which it reaches its full potential. Just as the butterfly goes through a metamorphosis, transformational leaders commit to a similar process that involves lifelong learning and change.

Change and upheaval in governments and institutions have accelerated and become today's way of life. Within this state of rapid change and chaos, leadership grapples to maintain a clear sense of vision when what's beyond the horizon is not always clear. Also, followers have become disillusioned with leadership in general and don't see how they can lead the organization to anything but a dismal or uncertain future. The challenge for today's leaders is to create a vision that can be modeled and articulated for an organization, thus making it possible for as many as possible to buy into creating stability and equity amid instability and inequity. It is an absolute priority for leaders to commit to personal development that isn't just head knowledge but a transformational journey.

When leaders go through the stages of life's metamorphosis, it expands and educates their worldview so they can adapt to the endless waves needed to adapt and grow. This metamorphosis transforms leaders into lighthouses that guide their organizations to navigate the rocky shoreline of change. Thus, I suggest the absence of transformational leadership in diversity programs is a key reason why those initiatives fail in many organizations.

Joseph Rost's (1991) classic and ground-breaking definition for leadership is:

> an influence relationship among leaders and followers who intend real change that reflects their mutual purpose (p. 102).

Diversity programs without influencing relationships are prone to fail. Leadership's commitment to produce change among staff through influence is a characteristic of transformational leadership that is absolutely essential in diversity programs. When leaders themselves commit to inward growth and transformation, it will prevent an ideology of diversity that is all talk and no substance. An organization energized by evolving leadership mindsets will ignite the flames of a twenty-first-century innovative workplace—among leaders *and* followers. Diversity leaders who can influence through relationships within their organizations will achieve the stated purpose of ID Transformation.

The influence component for the transformational leadership building block is essential for changing any failing DEI program into an ID Transformation one. The underlying historical causes of inequities within organizations can and will hinder the development of an authentic sense of belonging. It takes the influence of a transformational leader to prune the cultural branches that prevent growth and provide vision that transforms hearts and minds.

Peter Northouse (2015) defines transformational leadership as:

> A process that changes and transforms people. It is concerned with emotions, values, ethics, standards, and long-term goals. It includes assessing followers' motives, satisfying needs, and treating them as fellow human beings (p. 161).

To undertake the journey toward ID Transformation, Northouse's definition of transformational leadership must be at the forefront of any organization's diversity program.

Northouse's (2015) references to leadership are based on the work of Bernard Bass, the developer of the transformational leadership concept. Along with his definition of transformational leadership, Bass provided four functional characteristics. These characteristics must be present when working toward organizational ID Transformation:

1. Idealized influence

2. Inspirational motivation

3. Intellectual stimulation

4. Individualized consideration

Let me explain these four characteristics and you will

understand why they and transformational leadership are so vital to the cause outlined in this book. First, *idealized influence* occurs when leadership models ID Transformation in such a way that the staff desires to emulate what they see or disengage from the process. *Inspirational motivation* takes place when leaders help staff catch the vision and become passionate about adopting inclusivity behaviors that create a culture of belonging. *Intellectual stimulation* occurs when leaders recognize the potential and value within the staff to be collaborators and contributors toward establishing a culture of ID Transformation. Finally, *individualized consideration* causes leaders to discover the hidden talents, understand life-shaping experiences, and provide learning resources that affect ID Transformation for staff.

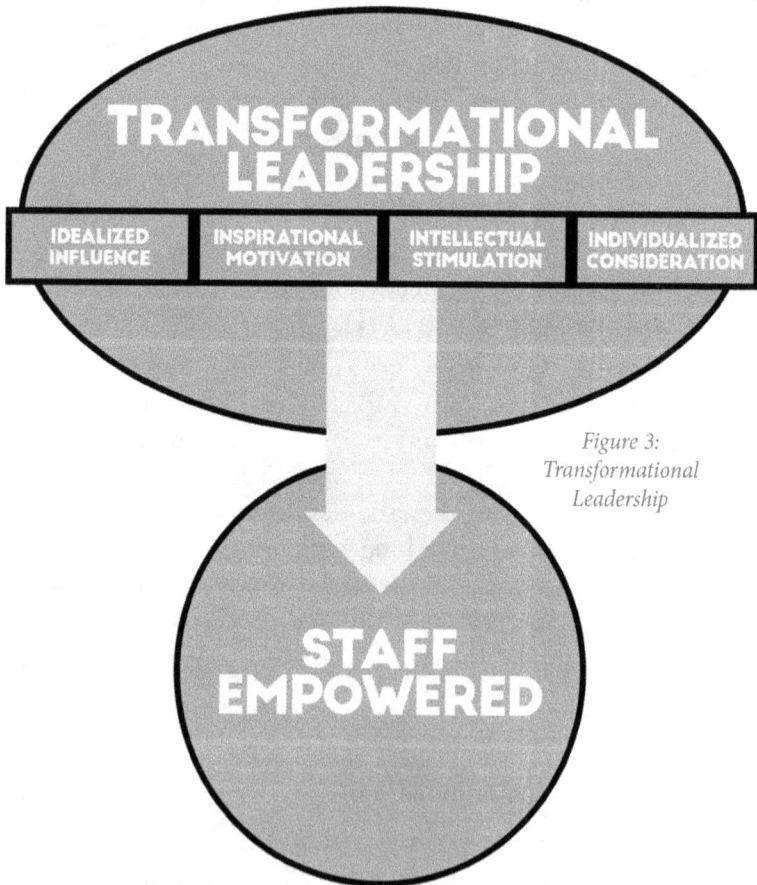

Figure 3:
Transformational
Leadership

Now you can see why this leadership style is so vital to influence change initiative. It starts with leadership that empowers followers and staff as depicted in Figure 3.

What would happen if organizations made transformational leadership qualities both espoused values *and* underlying assumptions in their culture? If that would happen, DEI programs would be transformed into ID Transformation programs, producing the intended organizational outcomes of increased proficiency and innovation—as well as a culture of belonging that would release the potential and creativity in the individuals involved.

CRITICAL-THINKING EXERCISE

Based on the four transformational leadership characteristics, rate your influential presence within your organization. Everyone in an organization influences their environment through the roles they serve and the presence they establish. Think about your role and how you impact influence, motivation, stimulation, and consideration. Rate yourself from 5 (highest) and 1 (lowest):

1. *Idealized influence* occurs when leadership models ID Transformation in such a way that the staff desires to emulate what they see or disengage. Circle your **influence** rating:

   5   4   3   2   1

2. *Inspirational motivation* takes place when leaders help staff catch the vision and become passionate about adopting inclusivity behaviors that create a culture of belonging. Circle your **motivation** rating:

   5   4   3   2   1

3. *Intellectual stimulation* occurs when leaders recognize the potential and value within the staff to be collaborators and contributors toward establishing a culture of ID Transformation. Circle your **stimulation** rating:

   5   4   3   2   1

4. *Individualized consideration* causes leaders to discover the hidden talents, understand life-shaping experiences, and provide learning resources that

affect ID Transformation for staff. Circle your **consideration** rating:

5   4   3   2   1

Most leaders have the hard skills required for daily administrative duties. Influential leaders lead with both hard *and* soft skills. This exercise focuses on a leader's soft skills necessary for transformational leadership. These skills empower and equip staff to follow and contribute to the organizational vision.

Challenge Your Leadership Skills

Based on your transformational leadership character rating, think about ways to improve your influence, motivation, stimulation, and consideration that will transform those who follow you.

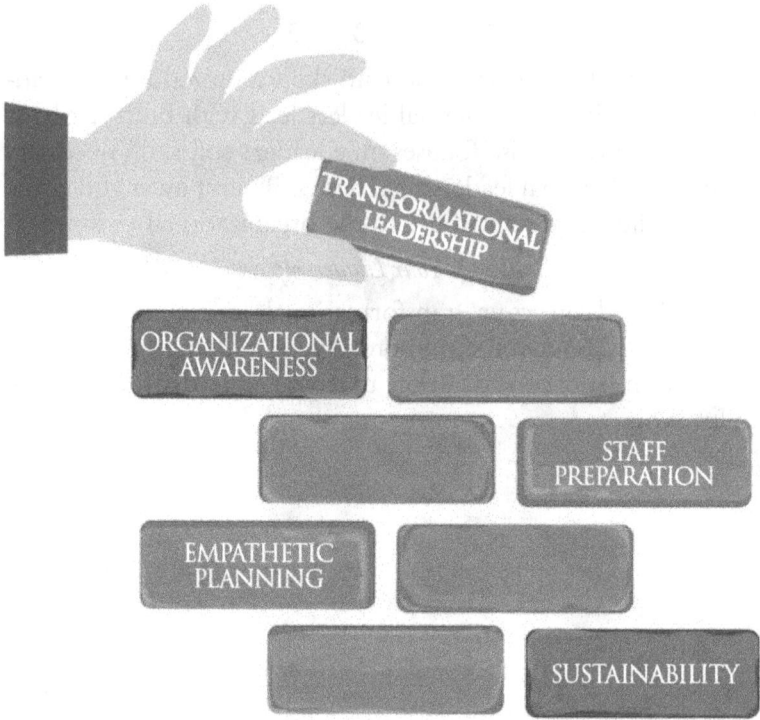

CHAPTER 6

WORLDVIEW

"It is always good to explore the stuff you don't agree with, to try and understand a different lifestyle or foreign worldview. I like to be challenged in that way, and always end up learning something I didn't know."
– Laura Linney

My Practitioner's Lens
As I stated in chapters one and four, a manager's remark

that diversity was already in our organization's DNA is permanently etched in my memory. After thinking about that staff meeting conversation, I pondered how managers could come to that conclusion without examining the results from a Climate Survey and Workplace Experience Survey. Also, my eyes did not deceive me when it came to diversity within my organization. With more than 300 staff, there were no people of color on the management team and no more than ten black male and female staff.

What's more, I was the Diversity and Inclusion Program Manager and was not part of the managerial team that was developing a strategic plan for our organizational restructuring. Even with a doctorate in higher education management, it seemed I was still invisible and unwanted. If senior managers could not see the "elephant in the room," then it was understandable why their assessment of the culture was inaccurate and why diversity was not a significant part of the strategic plan.

Everyone, including managers and leaders has had life-shaping experiences that have influenced and shaped every individual's worldview. Managers who cannot see the "elephant in the room" or choose ignorance over truth can prevent their staff from ever realizing their fullest potential by confronting this restrictive worldview. As a result of personal biases shaped by learned social-cultural norms, individuals must work to understand their thinking about diversity. I am reminded of Neil Tyson's quote: "People have enough truth to think they are right, but not enough truth to know they are wrong."

If managers do not see the need to be intentional about expanding their worldview, it affects their managerial skills and creates negative workplace experiences because managers cannot help but influence their workplace according to their own worldviews. If a manager's cultural experiences have not contributed toward the development of an enlightened or broadened worldview, it can result in destructive workplace outcomes that affect staff productivity and morale.

Managers who invest in a growth mindset positively influence a workplace which in turn enhances human and organizational advancement. In other words, managers can only lead staff as far as they themselves have gone. Thus, I present the worldview component in this chapter to help leaders expand their cultural worldview.

Worldview Component

The main objective of this component is to establish a practical self-assessment cycle that includes evaluation, improvement, and assessment that helps leaders learn and grow personally so they can increase their influence. Maverick Rozwell (2019) states that 95% of individuals surveyed in a global study think they are self-aware and open-minded. However, the statistical evidence reveals that between 10% or 15% are actually self-aware.

Also, earlier research studies on organizational change disclosed that 20% of the people proactively seek change, while 80% never seek change unless forced to do so. These studies provide evidence that individuals lack not only the self-awareness but also the initiative to pursue personal growth. Their stagnant worldviews that are not evolving through new life experiences hinder realistic perspectives of self and others in a workplace environment, thus the need for investment in leadership development, as seen in Figure 4.

The evolution of their worldviews will prepare leaders for the adaptive challenges associated with building ID Transformational institutions. For this reason, an institutional coaching or mentoring program can assist leaders with a continuous process made up of three concepts critical to self-change: position, disposition, and reposition, which I define as follows:

1. The *position* is an evaluation process in which coaching helps leaders define and evaluate their current worldview which then determines a personalized development plan.

2. The *disposition* is an improvement process that takes leaders through the challenge of change by providing an action plan of new learning experiences to expand their worldview. The action plan consists of the following steps to guide leaders toward key performance indicators:

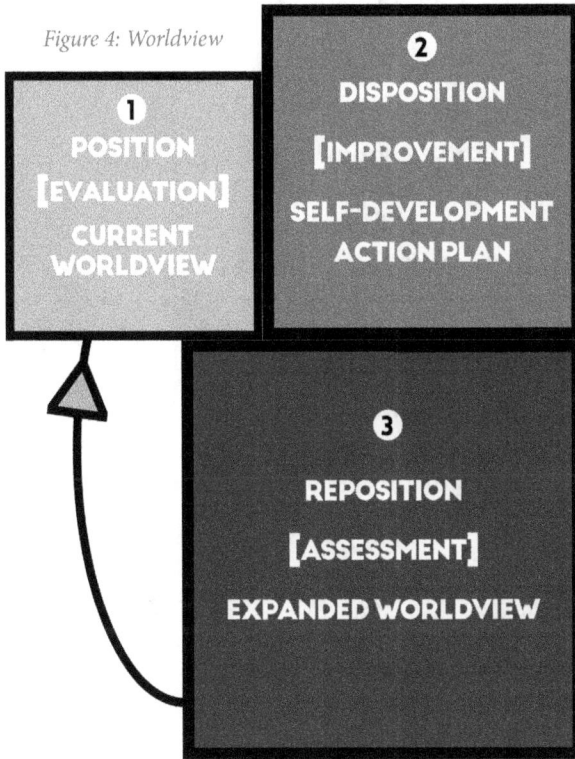

Figure 4: Worldview

- Develop a personalized action plan to engage broader life experiences.
- Define resources necessary to achieve growth outcomes.
- Establish accountability measures for said action plan.
- Set a target date for intended outcomes.
- Assess performance outcomes.
- Analyze key performance indicators (tangible objectives) for success or failure.

3. The *reposition* assesses the leader's intended change. Broadening a leader's worldview will

lead to positive expanded influence, thus creating an ID Transformational workplace, which results in leaders becoming better collaborators as they learn to value and respect diverse differences and viewpoints.

The pushback from attempts to embrace inclusivity and diversity can be subtle because they are rooted in institutional biases that stem from roots of social or cultural inequality. The diversity disparity that exists in many institutions is a paradox because these institutions are seen by many as progressive visionaries. Hence, institutions have an obligation to serve as examples that demonstrate the benefits of cultural diversity in their organization. However, diversity initiatives cannot be implemented without first understanding the reality of an institution's culture so that realistic learning and development plans can be devised to address underlying and often invisible causes of inequity.

How do leaders go from comprehending and desiring diversity practices to applying them? I would suggest that a diversity program will help leaders see the need for such and then provide constructive platforms to guide leaders toward self-growth. Self-change is a necessity and provides the impetus and moral authority to influence efforts toward organizational change of any kind, especially that which embraces diversity practices.

Let's review for a minute. The worldview component lays out an accountability process for leaders to understand their worldview that expands through position, disposition, and reposition. The *position* is an evaluation process in which coaching helps leaders define and evaluate their current worldview which then determines a personalized development plan.

The *disposition* is an improvement process that takes leaders through the challenge of change by providing an action plan of new learning experiences that broaden their worldview. The *reposition* assesses the leader's intended change.

My worldview component for building block two guides leaders through self-assessment to enhance personal growth by expanding their worldview. Developing an inclusive culture that embraces diversity in institutions depends on leaders who seek opportunities to learn and widen their life experiences.

CRITICAL-THINKING EXERCISE

Reflect on how you can broaden your worldview to influence your organization as follows:

- Step one: Think about and define your personal worldview towards diversity.
- Step two: Think about situations that challenge your worldview toward diversity.
- Step three: Refer to Figure 4, reflect on how leadership can help expand their worldview where diversity is concerned.
- Step four: Think how you can help incorporate an ID Transformational worldview conducive to your institution.

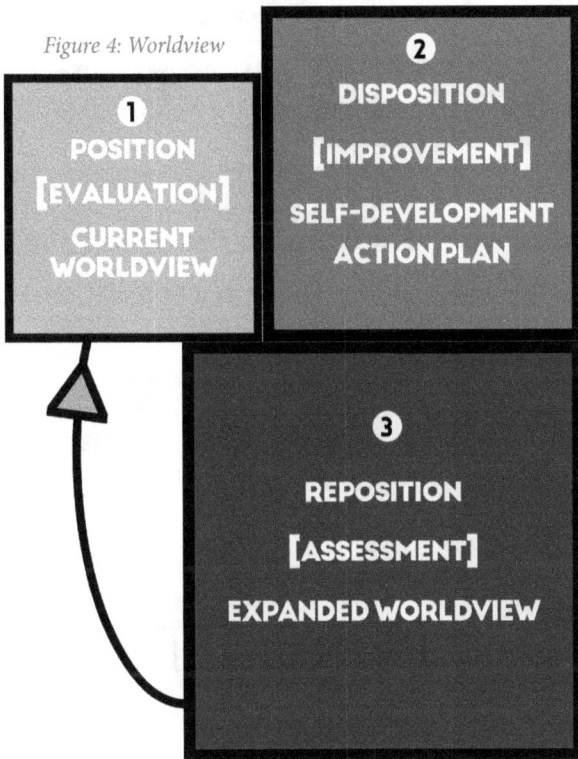

Figure 4: Worldview

1
POSITION
[EVALUATION]
CURRENT
WORLDVIEW

2
DISPOSITION
[IMPROVEMENT]
SELF-DEVELOPMENT
ACTION PLAN

3
REPOSITION
[ASSESSMENT]
EXPANDED WORLDVIEW

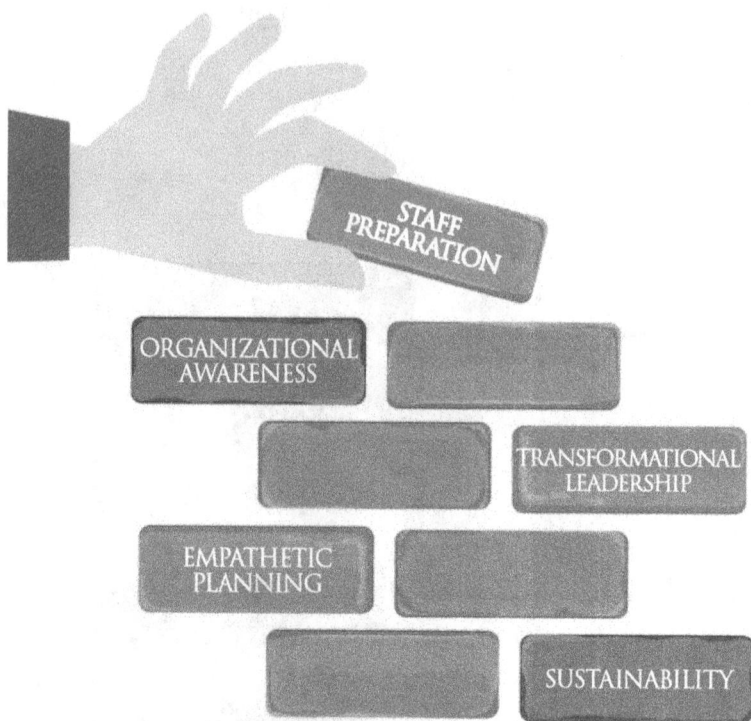

STAFF PREPARATION

ORGANIZATIONAL AWARENESS

TRANSFORMATIONAL LEADERSHIP

EMPATHETIC PLANNING

SUSTAINABILITY

CHAPTER 7

PURPOSE

"The purpose of human life is to serve, and to show compassion and the will to help others." – Albert Schweitzer

My Practitioner's Lens

I admire family, friends, and associates who seemed to have a sense of purpose. My interactions with them give me an understanding of their motivation and commitment to learn, grow, and serve. I was always amazed by their insights and empowered by being in their presence. Their life mission and accomplishments were a bit intimidating but at the same time inspirational examples to assist me in my own life journey.

What inspired me most about the professional mentors in my life was their thirst for learning. Their accomplishments in higher education did not allow them to lose sight of the need to retain a teachable spirit. I was empowered when they had a listening ear to learn even from me. Because they were committed to learning and development, they were not motivated by accolades and did not rest on their laurels. Instead, their inner drive and strength connected them to the empowerment of purpose.

When I saw the power in their purpose, I desired to know if I had a purpose in life or was simply allowing life circumstances to direct my path. I must confess that examining myself for purpose was a challenge. I was aware of my personal, academic, and professional interests and skills but had no clue as to if and how they connected to my purpose. Not until I had an opportunity to teach a course on *Finding Life Purpose* did I understand how my life-shaping experiences, skills, talents, and passion were all road signs that led to my purpose discovery. In preparation to teach others about discovering their life purpose, I began putting together the pieces of my own purpose puzzle.

Two life situations that magnified and clarified my purpose were attending a leadership conference and reading evaluations from technology classes I taught. At a city leadership conference, several individuals gave testimonies regarding innovative programs implemented at their organization. Listening to the testimonies, I noticed that each speaker had a life purpose which helped them develop innovative ideas. I was so impressed with the presentations that I turned to a colleague and said, "I wish I had a purpose like the presenters."

Her immediate response was, "You do. You walk alongside people to teach, counsel, and encourage." My colleague's insightful response helped me recognize that my purpose was so close—so second-nature—that I had somehow missed it. I was so deep into the forest that I could not see the trees. When purpose becomes a matter of habit, we don't see or appreciate it. Like driving a car or brushing our teeth, we don't need to think about it; we just unconsciously do it.

Another eye-opening experience where purpose was concerned was once when I worked in technology alongside many bright technical experts. I felt challenged not being as technologically savvy as they were. Even though I had received many excellent evaluations from years of instructor surveys from my class and workshop registrants, I was still oblivious to my strengths and success. Finally, I realized those surveys provided much insight into my purpose.

I did not understand the feedback I had received because I was focusing on not being as technically competent as other analysts and presenters. I missed seeing that I was working more on the practical side of technology, creating and teaching technology in ways that people could grasp. My approach to training provided practical ways for technically-challenged individuals to comprehend what many technical analysts couldn't convey.

I learned from discovering my purpose not to compare my abilities to others but to look inward at and focus on my own competencies (another aspect of self-awareness). When staff in an organization understand their need to tap into their strengths and skills, they will discover the power source only purpose can provide.

Purpose Component

If I ask you, the reader, to define your purpose, you may or may not be able to do so. As an instructor and practitioner, I had numerous conversations with students and peers who struggled to discover their life purpose, wondering if it existed or had any relevance to their career. When individuals understand their purpose in life, however, it helps them connect their life mission to their work and to others.

The purpose component for Building Block Staff Preparation is vital for staff and organizational advancement. A person unaware of their purpose is like a leaf fallen from a tree and then driven wherever the wind blows. Many people in organizations are like that leaf, tossed about and not knowing their destination or the reason for getting there. If we add the leaves of other staff and leaders to theirs, the pile can become quite large. Let me give you an example.

One day a colleague and I walked to the parking garage together at the end of the day. During that time, she mentioned her dissatisfaction at work. Her manager constantly assigned random and uninteresting projects that didn't align with her job description. Being confused over what her exact job position was, she requested a meeting with the manager regarding her career direction.

I asked if she knew her purpose and professional interests and she responded that she did not. Before requesting a meeting with the manager, I advised her to clarify possible career goals that aligned with her interests, skills, and passion. I also told her she should not put her confidence in feedback from someone unaware of her value or hidden talents. It was futile to give her manager permission to advise her on a professional path when the manager had limited awareness of her purpose and professional goals.

My doctoral dissertation topic was "Influence of Productivity Software on Staff Development." One of the questions that guided my research was, "What findings were unexpected?" One such finding was how often staff were left alone to figure out what development they needed. Their leaders required and valued staff development but gave no input and allotted no time for professional development. I also found it odd that the organization's annual performance appraisal had no formal development plan or accountability procedures.

A transformational leader would be more apt to collaborate with their staff in developing an action plan for personal and professional development that aligns with a person's purpose. Staff equipped to perform their job duties without understanding their purpose are prevented from achieving to their fullest potential. Purpose gives a person the incentive to take their skillset to another level of mastery that will significantly impact organizational innovation. Furthermore, life purpose is part of the discovery process for the following:

1. Understanding how life-shaping experiences
   have served to develop ideas of self and others.

2. Realizing talents, skills, and passion.

3. Motivation to pursue lifelong learning.

4. Recognizing life's purpose is larger than self.

5. Identifying with one's need for an interdependent community.

6. Knowing one's professional mission.

To avoid the blowing leaf scenario, leaders must collaborate with staff and provide resources to guide their development program. An ID Transformational organization exists when leaders work to uncover hidden talents and interests in the staff's work-life well-being. This also bridges the superior-subordinate gap to increase workplace productivity and innovation.

Purpose provides a sense of direction in life and increases one's professional effectiveness. To provide a personal context regarding purpose, I declined the initial offer when approached about the new Diversity and Inclusion Program Manager position as mentioned in the Introduction. The reason for my decision was a passion for increasing my effectiveness in student, faculty, and staff professional development. My purpose as a learning specialist in technology was fulfilled because I could develop and teach training programs in a practical way that allowed individuals to comprehend the use and value of technology. Therefore, I declined the position because I desired to continue this career path. After being given time to think about the new position, however, I realized it connected to my purpose, would provide unique learning opportunities, and would broaden my impact on the institutional mission.

CRITICAL-THINKING EXERCISE

The purpose component for the Building Block Staff Preparation is a significate part of strengthening individual and organizational capacity for progressive innovation. This critical thinking exercise enables you to align your life's purpose with your institution's mission. There are numerous resources to guide you through a more extensive process of self-discovery, but I created this exercise specifically to reveal life purpose and career direction. Let's start by having you answer these three questions:

1. Who am I?

2. What is my life's purpose?

3. Where do I want to be in my professional career?

Most of the people I ask those questions have difficulty providing answers. If that's true for you, then the following critical thinking exercises will get you thinking more about how to answer.

The who question reveals who you are (or are not).

Four aspects of your being can help explain who you are: environment, personality type, talent, and passion.

- The *environment* has an impact on who you are. Think about how the following environmental influences have impacted who you are: family, friends, relationships, and schools.

- *Personality Type:* Various personality tests reveal temperaments, such as the Myers-Briggs

Type Indicator and Enneagram. The OCEAN Personality Traits are also suitable for this critical thinking exercise. From the OCEAN big five personality traits (Flexmr, 2021) below, think about what trait is the most accurate description of your personality type:

> *Openness*—Sometimes called intellect or imagination, this represents your willingness to try new things and think outside the box. Expressions of this type include insightfulness, originality, and curiosity.

> *Conscientiousness*—This trait is characterized by your desire to be careful, diligent, and delay immediate gratification with self-discipline. Common expressions include ambition, discipline, consistency, and reliability.

> *Extroversion*—This category would have you draw energy from others and seeks social connections or interaction instead of being alone (introversion). Extrovert traits include being outgoing, energetic, and confident.

> *Agreeableness*—This measures how an individual interacts with others which determines their compassion and cooperation. The most prevalent expressions of this trait include tactfulness, kindness, and loyalty.

> *Neuroticism*—This trait manifests itself in a tendency towards negative personality traits, emotional instability, and self-destruction.

- *Talents*: These are the skills and expertise you rely on to do a job or task. Think about your skill set in the following areas: job, life, and sports.

- *Passion:* These are the things in life that stimulate, intrigue, or motivate you to action or involvement. The following questions can help reveal life passion:
    ◆ What motivates you?
    ◆ What issues draw your attention?
    ◆ What makes you lose track of time?
    ◆ What do you want to accomplish?
    ◆ What angers you?

The what question reveals life purpose

Use the insights from your environment, personality type, talents, and passion answers to answer the following questions.

- Who are you?
- Where do you belong?
- When do you feel fulfilled?

The where question reveals life mission

The following questions will help you develop a mission statement.

- What is important to you?
- Where do you want to go?
- What does "the best" look like to you?
- What kind of legacy do you want to leave behind?

This critical thinking section proposes three questions

1. Who am I?
2. What is my life's purpose?
3. Where do I want to be in my professional career?

The purpose for answering these questions is to help you draft your purpose and mission statement. Here is an example of my statement to help you draft yours.

My mission statement reflects the words of Dr. Martin

Luther King Jr.: "Everybody can be great because anybody can serve. You only need a heart full of grace. A soul generated by love." *Thus, my life mission is to develop a heart full of grace and a soul generated by love that will enrich and empower the lives of others.* I strive to accomplish this mission by the following objectives:

- to seek and establish a meaningful relationship with God,
- to discover and accept who I am,
- to develop my life purpose,
- to enrich my life and the lives of others that cross my path,
- to share my heart's passion through helping, teaching, and mentoring others,
- to maintain a humble and teachable spirit.

Note: After reading my mission statement and this chapter on purpose, the definition between purpose and mission can be subjective if you are wondering about the difference. Some individuals would suggest both are synonymous. My perspective on mission and purpose is this: Mission gives me direction or focus (tangible objectives), and purpose is who I am from birth and is connected to life experiences, personality, talents, and passion. Thus, my mission aligns with who I am (purpose: to serve). I developed this critical exercise from this understanding.

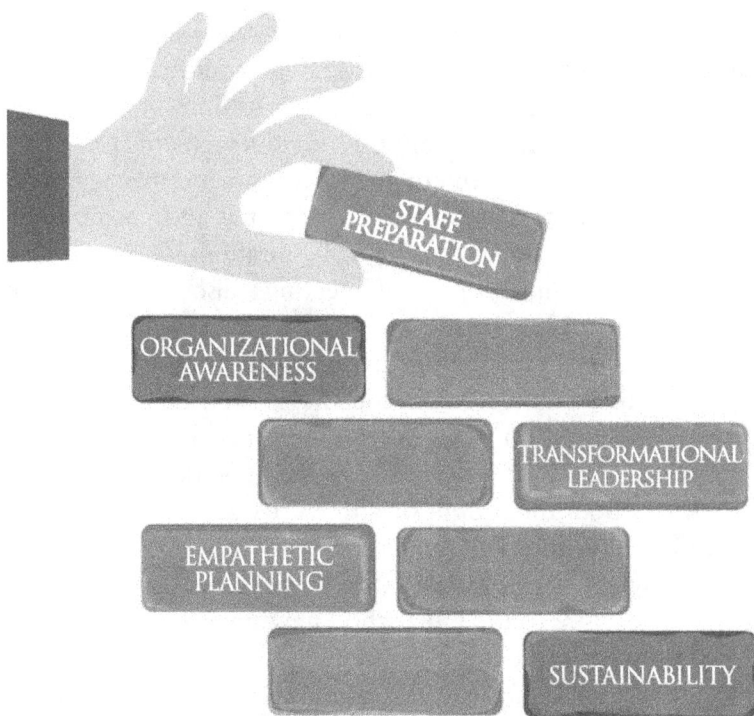

ORGANIZATIONAL AWARENESS

STAFF PREPARATION

TRANSFORMATIONAL LEADERSHIP

EMPATHETIC PLANNING

SUSTAINABILITY

CHAPTER 8

ADVANCEMENT

"Every enterprise is a learning and teaching institution. Training and development must be built into it on all levels, training, and development that never stop."
– Peter Drucker

My Practitioner's Lens

During my work experience in an institutional division comprised mostly of white males, I told you how I felt invisible and underutilized, and I also suppressed potential talents and abilities. I was not always aware of those potentials despite my commitment to the organization and my work ethic to do my best. I pursued accomplishments like advanced degrees and professional training with little encouragement from managers. When I sought new professional opportunities, it was without my direct manager's input or encouragement. I wonder what my career advancement could have been if managers had made the effort to see my hidden potential and championed my cause toward higher professional aspirations?

At my annual appraisal meetings, also known as the performance review, I always inquired as to how I could prepare for new or unseen opportunities relative to organizational changes, but never received a specific answer. The managerial appraisals focused on my work performance without any attempts to discover or develop my hidden potential.

Without their input or interest, I was left alone to plan my career direction. The only times that I advanced in my career was when I took the initiative and bypassed a manager to express my desire to the CIO who knew my potential and saw me beyond my current job description.

Along with a lack of managerial collaboration towards professional advancement, there were also experiences of biases. One such experience was early in my career when a new manager took the time to observe my job performance and then met with me to inform me of their concern regarding my previous manager's unfavorable assessment of my performance.

My new manager felt the previous manager's opinion was biased because my job performance and commitment were exceptional. What makes managerial biases disheartening is that there is no accountability for their actions if and when they suppress staff development or if they are being disingenuous about their desire to empower their staff. These managerial infractions also occurred with other staff, people who had great potential but who needed support.

When managers and supervisors are unaware of their biases and unable to see staff beyond their job description, it hinders increased organizational capacity and professional advancement. Leadership has the responsibility to encourage and empower staff to aspire to realize their full potential, thus providing learning and development opportunities that benefit professional efficacy and meet the demands of an ever-changing environment. I can only imagine what could have been if managers had observed me and then collaborated with me concerning my professional growth. I would then have been more empowered to empower others.

Advancement Component

I derived the advancement component from my dissertation research on "The Influence of Productivity Software on Staff Development." The staff interviews from my research revealed there was no collaboration or development plan with their leadership to keep up with the constant changes in the productivity software. Those I interviewed were overwhelmed trying to keep up with the latest software and therefore defaulted to using older software versions. Most were left to navigate their professional development without supervisor or management assistance. However, the managers paid lip service to valuing new learning but then did nothing to assist staff with a development plan to increase workplace proficiency or prepare for career advancement.

The astounding pace of change creates unique adaptive challenges for staff to remain professionally savvy. The investment in staff development demonstrates an organization's appreciation for the value of staff and a commitment to advocating for staff and workplace advancement. The advancement component is a partnership model that supports individualized staff development in hard and soft skills.

The component for advancement in this chapter is an evaluation and assessment tool to promote learning and development. This component is also guided by assessment coaching with the intent to increase workplace competency. This type of coaching is an essential component to assist staff with a personalized action plan for staff learning and development.

The goal of assessment coaching is to measure proficiency levels in the workplace and then debrief staff as to how to navigate the available professional tools, resources, and services to personalize a development action plan. An assessment

61

plan's development will determine both an individual's professional strengths and also the learning needed to establish goals and development objectives. The assessment coach also measures development outcomes for proficiency in both hard and soft skills associated with a development plan's continuance.

The advancement component can also be part of an institution's annual appraisal program as a collaborative endeavor that is a non-threatening approach for staff advancement. Figure 5 illustrates a process for staff advancement.

The advancement component addresses the following factors to facilitate staff advancement:

1. *Mission*: Making sure that the learning and development plan aligns with the workplace and institutional mission.

2. *Objectives*: Evaluate learning and development needs for the workplace, seek the appropriate resources, and set competency standards.

3. *Improvement*: Develop an improvement plan to help master and apply skills by maximizing strengths and minimizing weaknesses.

4. *Assessment*: Examine strengths and weaknesses that result from the improvement plan.

5. *Outcomes*: Measure competency outcomes demonstrated in the workplace.

Organizational growth expectations will not be successful if staff are not engaged in constant learning and development. Training programs are essential for maintaining an inclusive culture that nurtures skills contributing to professional efficacy. When an organization establishes development as a vital part of their culture, staff will feel a part of the institutional mission. Creating an ID Transformation culture consists of all staff being part of the following institutional learning and development practices:

1. Fostering training that is in alignment with the institutional-at-large and departmental missions.

2. Encouraging leader and staff buy-in and

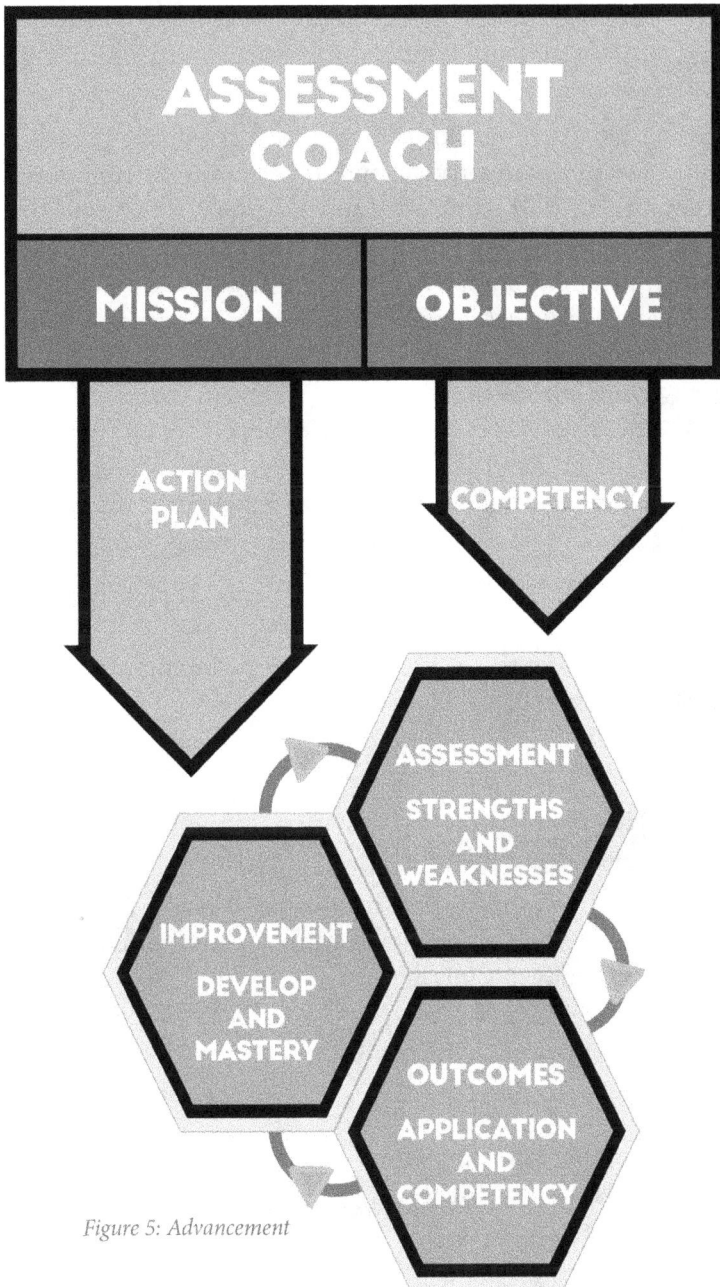

Figure 5: Advancement

cooperation toward relevant training.

3. Supporting ongoing learning and development that enhance hard and soft skills.

Michael Seibold (2015) argues training is critical to provide staff with the skills that support continual growth required for job performance, and are essential for monitoring and evaluating staff knowledge and expertise. My advancement component is a model for such a learning and development program. Training initiatives for an organization's culture serve to enhance *relational-interconnected individuals causing a palpable sense of belonging that increases human and organizational capacity for progressive innovation.*

Because of the unique adaptive challenges for organizations caused by rapid change, innovative learning programs are key to the enhancement of staff advancement. My learning and development program consists of two modules: staff advancement and enrichment.

Staff Advancement

A training program aims to provide learning and development that broaden knowledge and mastery of both soft and hard skills, thus, contributing to productive work experiences and professional development.

1. Learning: Learning resources should include internal and external learning platforms for:

- job shadowing (on-the-job training is when an employee observes another employee's job performance to develop new skills)
- staff internships
- HR learning and development
- lunch and learn
- workshops that include professional development and
- work-life balance
- conferences

- online resources (example: LinkedIn Learning an on-demand instructional videos to develop workplace skills)
- workplace training

2. *Development*: Development should encompass:

- A staff empowerment plan that provides action steps that strengthen workplace skills.
- A personalized staff career path through certifications and degree advancement.

3. Coaching

A coaching program provides an essential asset for learning and development because of the ever-changing workplace skill requirements. The program's personalized professional development planning helps staff navigate the maze of overwhelming learning options. The goal is to also assist staff through a non-threatening approach by both one-on-one professional development coaching and small-group professional development support.

Staff Enrichment

The learning and development program will proactively build a workplace of inclusion that establishes a culture valuing an ID transformation, resulting in the following behavioral practices: connect, respect, contribute, and embrace. The aim is to initiate interdependence among staff with various professional and life experiences in a collaborative effort for institutional advancement.

Inclusion

A diverse workforce in an inclusive environment improves individual and organizational performance, providing better value to constituents. Every employee will feel welcome and motivated to be more creative and productive when the following are done:

- Form an inclusion team that oversees the development of employee initiatives to promote a workplace experience of belonging.

- Create and manage communication platforms related to staff inclusion initiatives such as staff onboarding and employee resource groups.

Diversity

Being intentional about maintaining and seeking a good cross-section of all people groups with different backgrounds and progressive mindsets will broaden organizational creativity and human capacity. Increasing diversity in the workplace provides new ways of thinking that will help your institution realize its full potential in achieving its mission through the following methods and people groups:

- hiring practices that are non-biased;
- partnerships with people groups comprised of people with disabilities, women in the workplace, people of color, LGBTQIA+, veterans, etc.;
- internships that provide opportunities in seeking and equipping new hires through community initiatives;
- collaboration with various diversity networks to share and support best practices and challenges.

The staff advancement training initiative helps staff master their current skills and develop new knowledge. Staff enrichment should be part of a training plan to establish and value an ID Transformational learning culture.

My advancement component is also a partnership forum so staff can work with their supervisor or manager on a personalized learning and development plan. Investment in staff development demonstrates an institution's appreciation for personal and professional growth. Imagine the unseen impact and unprecedented innovation that is waiting to be unleashed within an organization that embraces input from diverse growth mindsets.

Alignment With The Organization

For organizations to achieve the full benefits from staff advancement, they must also understand organizational alignment that helps every staff's professional mission to align with the organizational mission. Staff advancement is a vital asset that ignites organizational ingenuity. No matter their roles, staff must understand how their professional mission and development aligns and impacts the institution-at-large. In many situations, staff focus on their duties and miss how their professional mission can significantly impact the organizational mission. Staff cannot afford to have tunnel vision that is task-oriented only but must have a broader perspective of how their professional contribution and development aligns with the institutional mission and values.

Figure 6 illustrates my idea of the process involving the staff's professional mission impacted by learning and development that increases staff and organizational capacity.

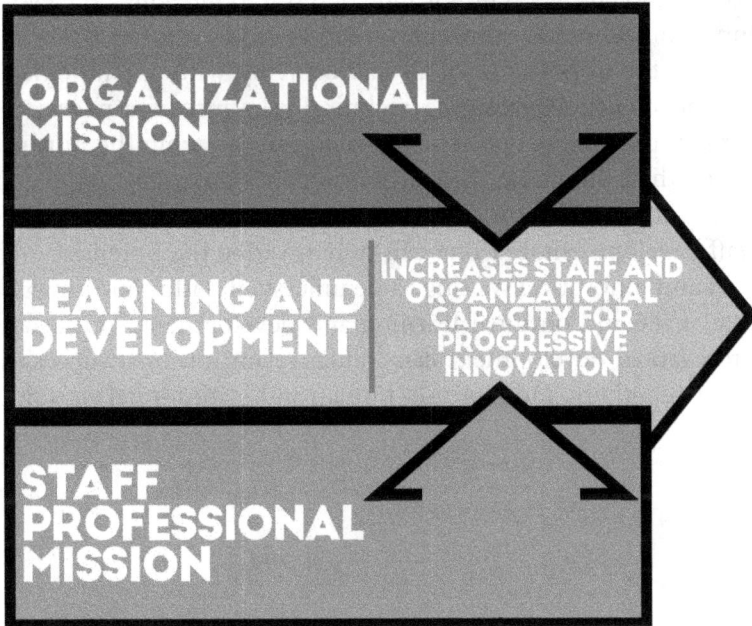

Figure 6: Alignment With The Organization

John Kennedy (2020) stated endeavors are not sufficient without purpose and direction. Hence, the alignment of organizational mission and staff professional mission must be central to organizational purpose and direction.

An inclusive culture that creates a safe and nurturing environment for fostering learning and development will increase collaboration and proficiency to meet an institution's changing needs. Staff who are committed to the institution's mission, values, and self-development experience positive outcomes within themselves and their work initiatives. As institutions enter new professional frontiers, equipped staff will share the adventures while contributing to institutional excellence, sustainability, and relevance.

As a learning specialist for innovative student and staff administrative systems, I was responsible for developing and delivering training. Before the initial installation of *PeopleSoft* (student administrative system) and *Skype for Business* (communications platform), users were resistant because they were comfortable after years of using technology that had become obsolete. My training approach was to introduce the evolution of technology throughout the years at the institution and explain the importance of all staff evolving with technological advancements. Maintaining technical relevance was necessary for staff professional proficiency and growth within the institution—thus, the name *Alignment with the Organization*.

In conclusion, institutions can evolve without much staff development, but one can only imagine the potential impact and innovation waiting to be unleashed within institutions that invest in continual learning and development. Thus, staff professional development can influence institutional successes as it strengthens and increases human and institutional capacity.

CRITICAL-THINKING EXERCISE

No matter your role, it is essential for you to understand how your professional mission aligns with your institution's mission. Figure 6 provides a perspective for you to understand your relationship and impact on organizational evolution through professional development.

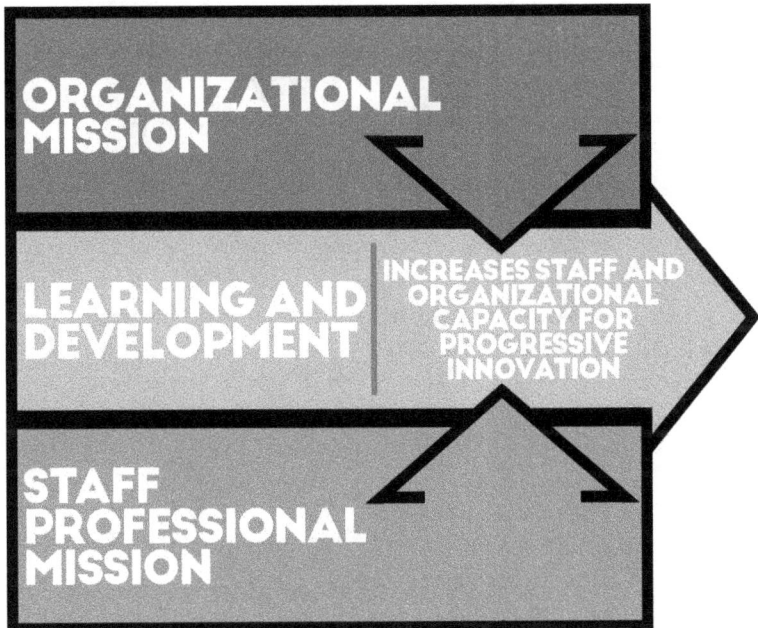

Figure 6: Alignment With The Organization

Examine your professional mission in relationship to the organization mission by taking the following steps:

- Step one: think about your professional mission.
  - List your talents and life skills.

- ◆ List things that motivate you in life.
- ◆ List your personal, educational, and professional goals.
- ◆ Reflect on your skills, motivations, and goals you listed.
- ◆ Write a professional mission statement consistent with your skills, motivations, and goals.
- Step two: Review your organization's mission and values statements.
- Step three: See if and where your professional mission statement aligns with your organization's mission statement. Where do they diverge?
- Step four: Think about how a professional development plan can support your professional mission.
- Step five: Develop an action plan for your professional development that align with your organization's mission.

Note: This critical-thinking exercise emphasizes the importance of *Alignment with the Organization*. As the organization evolves, your professional mission should be progressing as well.

ORGANIZATIONAL AWARENESS

EMPATHETIC PLANNING

TRANSFORMATIONAL LEADERSHIP

STAFF PREPARATION

SUSTAINABILITY

CHAPTER 9

STRATEGY

"The relevance of strategy, people, processes, structure, leadership and everything else in a company is determined by the extent to which they contribute to the creation of a product."
– Michael Kouly

My Practitioner's Lens
Throughout my tenure in higher education, I experienced many reorganizations and new departmental initiatives

that required strategic planning. On occasion, there were planning sessions that included all staff input. During many of these planning meetings, I would hear from staff that they felt managers were disingenuous about organizational buy-in because managers did not consider their ideas.

The staff concerns with misrepresented buy-in became a reality during a departmental restructuring when I served as the Diversity and Inclusion Program Manager. A senior leadership team led the strategy efforts for the restructuring. After developing a proposal, the team shared it with all staff for input. Leaders requested that staff submit action items that the restructuring team may have omitted. After reviewing the proposal, I noticed nothing that addressed "the elephant in the room" — diversity, equity, and inclusion disparity. My response was our need to include DEI initiatives in the organizational restructuring. The strategic planning for restructuring was deficient without DEI included in the mission, values, and policy.

I received no response regarding my requested input. Also, the leadership team did not include the DEI suggestion in the proposal. I was certainly not alone, for I heard similar experiences from peers regarding their input. There were other times when management respectfully listened to suggestions but gave little or no feedback on ideas. Although manager advice and feedback were lacking at times, the experience helped me to develop building blocks for ID Transformation, along with my experiences in organizational training and development.

I was never sure if my ideas were flawed or if I simply was the wrong messenger with the right message. Either way, my managers seldom embraced my ideas for our inclusion program and what's more, seemed to have no motivation to involve themselves. Any initiative for a diversity program that does not have a leadership and staff partnership is doomed to failure.

Whenever leaders mandate a diversity program (or any program for that matter), they also have the responsibility to articulate and model the way that requires establishing a strategic plan. An organizational strategic plan is crucial for the development and implementation of a diversity program. This

Figure 7: Strategy

chapter's strategy component for building block four illustrates the factors necessary for launching a successful program.

Strategy Component

The strategy component for my empathetic planning building block reflects James Jaccard's (2010) description of a direct causal relationship in which one variable affects another variable's outcome. This variable comes about when one action leads to another action that is good or bad—similar to the ends justifying the means. The strategy component is based on the impact from an action that will produce a good or bad effect towards ID Transformation. Thus, each action item is vital in establishing a relevant diversity program.

Figure 7 shows action items that can be efficient or deficient, resulting in the consequences for a diversity program. During the development and implementation process for the strategy component, leaders should approach each action item with empathy regarding staff concerns and appreciation for their uniqueness within an organization. Also, when all the actions are efficient, well-organized, and in sync, the goals for a diversity program will produce favorable outcomes.

Leadership-Driven With Staff Involvement

Belonging is part of any diversity program vision. This vision starts with leaders articulating a new reality and then modeling the way that invites staff engagement. Successful diversity outcomes depend on leadership motivating staff throughout the entire process until behavioral practices become rooted in the culture. Gary Kramer (2010) emphasized the importance of leaders promoting a collaborative culture to achieve a common goal.

Mission, Values, And Policy

The mission, values, and policy must use clear and understandable terminology that describes the organization's intent. During the implementation process, the organizational mission, values, and policies are core action items to guide and establish meaningful diversity initiatives.

A Strategic Plan

The successful implementation of a diversity program depends upon effective strategic planning in which there is shared partnership between leaders and staff. Strategic planning assesses an organization's capacity, measuring strengths, weaknesses, opportunities, and threats while creating a more diverse organization. A strategic plan also aims to design valid parameters that address and support the adaptive challenges to implementing an effective diversity program.

Buy-In And Resources

Leadership and staff buy-in for any diversity program's mission is crucial. Also, resources are vitally important to maintain hope, purpose, and progress. The lack of necessary financial and human resources to sustain a diversity program will thwart outcomes and disappoint expectations, like a car without gas unable to reach its destination.

Creativity

Creativity is essential when developing innovative program initiatives tailored to each unique organizational culture. The ideas from leaders and staff are the start of envisioning an ideal culture of belonging. A diversity program involving the collective efforts of everyone's imagination, curiosity, motivation, and determination will generate ideas and discover hidden opportunities that can achieve unimagined accomplishments.

My strategy component illustrates the impact of institutional practices on the effectiveness of a diversity program. The synergy of mission, values, policy, buy-in, resources, strategic planning, and creativity are not independent, stand-alone actions. When institutional actions are deficient or function independently, they cannot achieve the standards set for any diversity program. Empathetic planning and creating efficient actions that are interdependent do not happen automatically. They require cooperation between all levels of the organization. What's more, there must be a harmonious connection between actions if a culture of ID Transformation is to be achieved. In other words, the right hand has to know what the left hand is doing, and the left hand cannot be fighting what the right hand initiates.

In summary, empathetic planning is necessary when working with different people groups. All actions within the strategy component should show empathy toward all staff. Leaders and diversity workers must consider, and address staff fears and competing interests during the development and implementation of a diversity program. When staff members are respected and included in the strategy actions, their contributions toward creating a culture of belonging will prove successful.

CRITICAL-THINKING EXERCISE

The strategy component for building block four describes an organizational process in which every action contributes to the achievement of an outcome. Think about how the strategy component can cause positive or negative effects in establishing a successful diversity program.

- Step one: Create a SWOT Analysis
    - Strength—List all the strengths within your organization that will support a diversity program.
    - Weakness—List all the weaknesses within your organization that will hinder a diversity program.
    - Opportunity—List all opportunities outside of your organization that will benefit your diversity program.
    - Threat—List all threats outside of your organization that can hinder your diversity program.
- Step two: Create a statement from the strengths and opportunities that reflect a healthy organizational culture relative to a diversity program.
- Step three: Create a statement from the weaknesses and threats that reflect an unhealthy organizational culture.
- Step four: Refer to Figure 7, think about how it can relate to your diversity program initiatives.
- Step five: From your strengths and opportunities

DEFICIENT ACTIONS CAUSE DEFICIENT DIVERSITY PROGRAMS

LEADERSHIP DRIVEN WITH STAFF INVOLVEMENT

MISSION, VALUES, POLICY

STRATEGIC PLAN

BUY-IN, RESOURCES

CREATIVITY

LEAD TO SUCCESSFUL DIVERSITY PROGRAMS

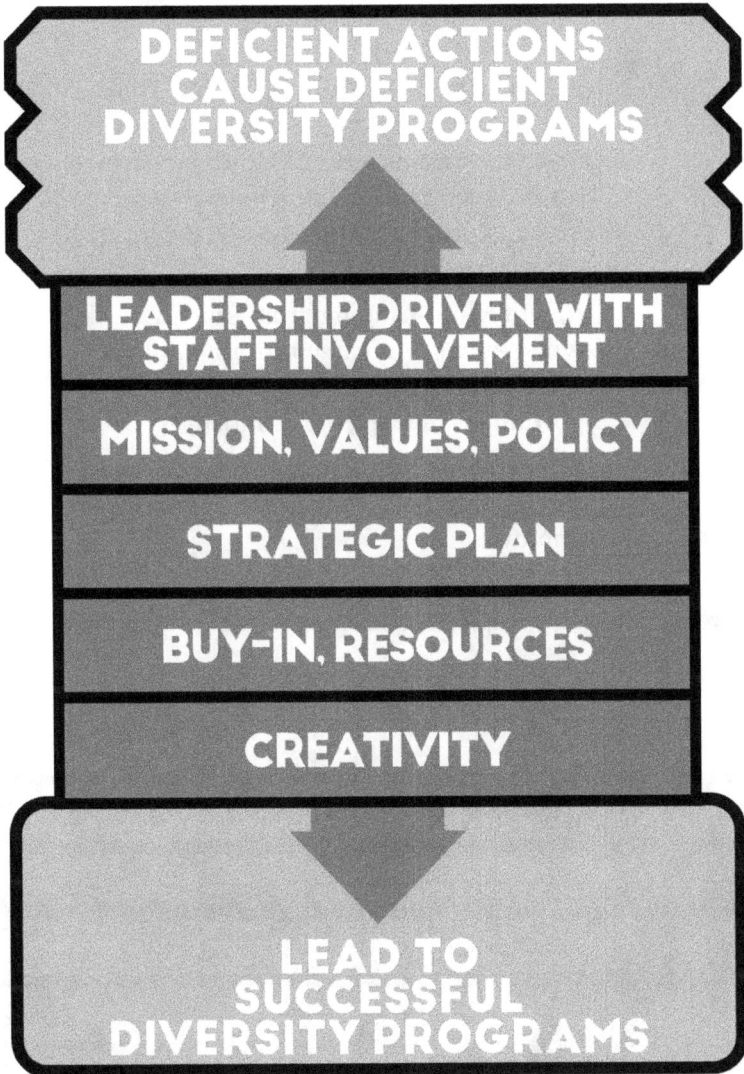

Figure 7: Strategy

statements, consider how positive impacts from mission, values, policy, buy-in, resources, strategic planning, and creativity can positively affect your diversity program.

- Step six: From your weaknesses and threats statements, consider how any negative influences from mission, values, policy, buy-in, resources, strategic planning, and creativity will negatively affect your diversity program.

- Step seven: Based on your SWOT analysis conclusion from steps five and six, create a practical approach to creating your diversity program initiatives (keep in mind incremental steps and prioritize by implementing one or two initiatives at a time).

  - Identify low-hanging fruit (initiatives that will not take much effort to implement) from your organizational strengths and opportunities to implement initiatives.

  - Prioritize your organization's weaknesses and threats, then select one or two issues to improve.

Once you have selected one or two program initiatives, develop a strategic implementation metric, or use the following metric:

BACKGROUND	ANSWER THE QUESTION "WHY ARE WE DOING THIS PROJECT?" OR "WHAT IS THE PRIMARY MOTIVATION?"
PROCESSES	IDENTIFY PROCESSES TO SUPPORT THE STRATEGIC GOAL. HOW WILL THE GOAL BE ACHIEVED?
BOUNDARIES	IDENTIFY SERVICES AND PROGRAMS THAT WILL BE AFFECTED BY THE IMPLEMENTATION PROCESS.
RISKS	WHAT ARE THE POTENTIAL PROBLEMS?
EXPECTED OUTCOME	WHAT IS THE DESIRED OUTCOME FOR THE INITIATIVE?
PERFORMANCE INDICATORS	HOW WILL THE EFFECTIVENESS OF THE INITIATIVE BE MEASURED?
RESPONSIBILITY	WHO WILL BE RESPONSIBLE FOR LEADING THE INITIATIVE?
TIMELINE	WHAT ARE THE START AND END DATES?

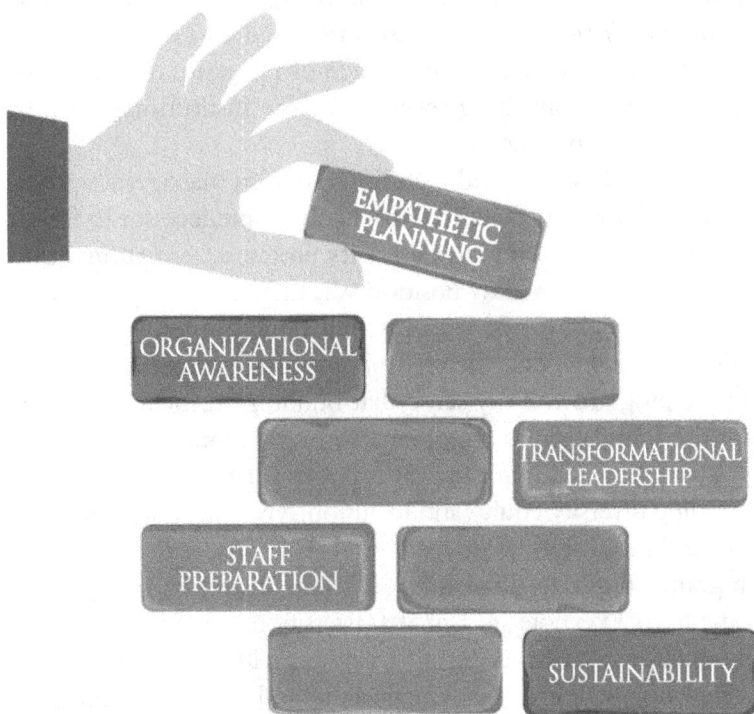

EMPATHETIC PLANNING

ORGANIZATIONAL AWARENESS

TRANSFORMATIONAL LEADERSHIP

STAFF PREPARATION

SUSTAINABILITY

CHAPTER 10

COLLABORATION

"Unity is strength… when there is teamwork and collaboration, wonderful things can be achieved."
– Mattie Stepanek

My Practitioner's Lens

As I mentioned previously, after receiving my doctoral degree in higher education management, I accepted a new position as Diversity and Inclusion Program Manager in my department of over 300 staff. The institution where I worked enrolled approximately 28,000 students and employed 5,000 faculty and 7,000 staff. The institution had an institution-wide diversity initiative, led by the Office of Diversity, that provided resources and consulting services for the institution's learning centers and departments.

The Diversity and Inclusion Program Manager was a new position in my department. Thus, I had no predecessor to follow, resulting in my developing a diversity program from ground zero. My first goal in my new position was to write a proposal for an inclusion program based on my collaboration component. My rationale for selecting the term *inclusion program* rather than diversity program was my sense that building an inclusive culture was the foundation for an organization to embrace diversity.

Before writing the proposal, I researched discussions surrounding diversity, equity, and inclusion. My main question after I read and heard from the experts was: How do I start an inclusion program unique to my workplace? The answer to my question came from a keynote speaker at a diversity retreat. His response to my question was "be creative." That was neither the answer I expected, nor did it give me a practical method to develop a program.

During my continued research on diversity, I realized that most information was based on theory without describing any clear processes for implementation. Not only was I unable to find a practical approach to setting up an inclusion program, but there was also no information about understanding cultural norms in an organization. I thought it necessary to comprehend the current organizational culture before developing an inclusion program, for how could we know how to get somewhere before we knew where we were? Builders do not build a new structure without laying the proper foundation. The same was true for building an inclusion program.

Eventually, I took the advice of the keynote speaker and became creative. After imagining how an inclusion program should look, I developed an inclusion proposal for my organization. This chapter's collaboration component for the Empathetic Planning Building Block comes from my proposal recommendation.

Collaboration Component

Organizations must be intentional if they desire to experience diversity, equity, and inclusion practices within their culture. An inclusion team is an effective means to develop and implement any organization's diversity program. Thus, my collaboration component outlines a cooperative approach emanating from a team that develops and oversees best practices for inclusion and diversity.

Team Approach

The collaboration component describes an inclusion team as a collective commitment among diverse leadership and staff from various departmental units. As the Diversity and Inclusion Program Manager, I led the inclusion team and served as the liaison between leaders and staff. There are three functional dynamics for an inclusion team: administrative, staff engagement, and networking.

1. Administrative efforts include:

   a. developing policies and a strategic plan for implementing, evaluating, assessing, and improving inclusion initiatives.

   b. coordinating inclusion initiatives by establishing various staff working groups such as professional development, communications, employee resources, innovation, and onboarding.

2. Staff engagement efforts include:

   a. providing relevant information platforms and participation activities that support inclusion.

   b. disseminating publications, announcements, and events for staff through media communications.

   c. soliciting and helping staff implement desired employee resource groups.

   d. providing staff-awareness training programs and resources regarding inclusion and diversity practices.

e. developing creative ways to engage staff in diversity awareness and celebrating the uniqueness of different ethnic people groups.

f. designing small groups that discuss topics relevant to diversity, equity, and inclusion issues.

g. setting up an inclusion focus group to research best practices for organizational advancement.

h. initiating one-on-one confidential sessions where staff express workplace questions, concerns, and issues relative to diversity, equity, and inclusion.

3. Network efforts include:

a. connecting with other institutional areas that are developing and implementing diversity programs. The network supports collaboration to share best practices and challenges that foster successful outcomes throughout the institution. It is also essential to work with the office of human resources and the office of diversity to establish meaningful partnerships and learning resources.

b. participating in external diversity networks to establish partnerships for support and guidance regarding new ideas and best practices related to the organization's diversity program.

My collaboration component for an inclusion team is a strategic approach to implement a unique diversity program for any organization. The process consists of three phases: administration, staff engagement, and network. The steps include practical approaches to address sensitive and challenging issues while attempting to change an organizational cultural mindset toward inclusive and diverse practices. The collaboration component for the Empathetic Planning Building Block is a joint venture among leaders and staff to establish a diversity program.

The adaptive challenge of becoming more inclusive has its barriers when attempting to change personal ideologies; thus, creating an inclusive culture must not be rushed but approached using thoughtful strategies and empathy toward behavioral change. Dia Mirza (2020) states, "It is critical for us to cultivate consciousness towards our environment, create awareness, galvanize people, and build sustainable innovations for sustainable development" (BrainyQuote.com).

As I mentioned previously, this collaboration component for building block four was a proposal outline for implementing a diversity program I created while serving as Diversity and Inclusion Program Manager. After soliciting and selecting members for an inclusion team, I presented a draft of the proposal at the first meeting when we discussed the team's purpose. After some discussion, the team unanimously accepted the proposal along with the suggestion to create an organizational mission statement for belonging. Creating the mission statement was a vital first step to guide the goals for our inclusion program.

When developing a mission statement for a diversity program, a team's or working group's first task is to understand the organizational culture. Chapter three provided a brief insight into cultural comprehension using Schein's three organizational culture levels: artifacts, espoused values, and underlying assumptions.

To define our workplace culture, the newly-established inclusion team conducted a group exercise to describe our existing culture along with an ideal culture of belonging. Each team member was given an assignment to write eight positive and negative adjectives that depicted the current workplace culture, with the rationale for their choices. Next, members wrote eight adjectives related to an ideal work culture of belonging and again provided their rationale. As a result of our group exercise, the team drafted a mission statement containing the adjectives consistent with a relevant inclusion program.

It is interesting that the team used mostly negative adjectives to describe the current organizational culture. Both positive and negative adjectives were helpful in developing a mission that reflected an ideal culture of belonging. The following mission statement was written by our inclusion team based on the team exercise:

> *Our department consists of diverse and knowledgeable individuals with different backgrounds, ideals, and mindsets. This dynamic provides innovative solutions and promotes a culture of inclusivity and a diverse working environment where individuals are valued, encouraged, and respected for their contributions. We do this by promoting awareness, actively listening, and embracing new ways of thinking. This cultivates a sense of belonging, encourages personal and professional development, and values every individual. We are then empowered to have a positive impact on those around us, while functioning cohesively from the belief that we are "one" to increase efficiency and productivity as we carry out the institution's mission.*

A mission statement serves as the guide in an organization's attempt to structure a practical vision, values, and diversity practice. My collaboration component is not static but nimble, capable of adapting to any organization's personality that is shaped by diverse mindsets and backgrounds—or lack thereof. Hence, a diversity program's mission provides clues as to what is essential for an ideal culture of belonging.

CRITICAL-THINKING EXERCISE

Take time to think about how to create an inclusion team for your diversity program that nurtures a culture of belonging while shaping and transforming various mindsets.

- Step one: List ways your organization is currently creating an inclusive workplace.
- Step two: List other ways your organization can become more inclusive.
- Step three: List participants, goals, and administrative responsibilities needed to enhance your diversity program.
- Step four: From your list, consider how you can create an inclusion team for your organization.
- Step five: Think about how to collaborate with others to improve diversity initiatives that increase workplace belonging.
- Step six: Think about an action plan to work with other staff and leaders to direct behaviors toward belonging.

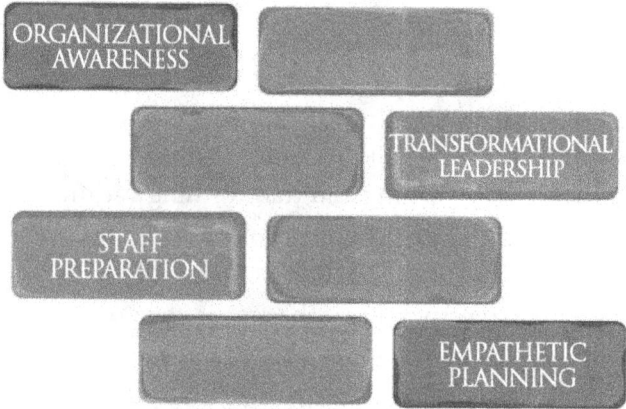

SUSTAINABILITY

ORGANIZATIONAL
AWARENESS

TRANSFORMATIONAL
LEADERSHIP

STAFF
PREPARATION

EMPATHETIC
PLANNING

CHAPTER 11

CONSISTENCY

*"We must shift our thinking away from short-term gain toward
long-term investment and sustainability, and always have the
next generations in mind with every decision we make."*
- Deb Haaland

My Practitioner's Lens

The most meaningful relationships in my life took time
and consistency to develop. Relationships are like a journey over

hills and through valleys. There are twists and turns, rough and smooth patches, getting lost then finding your way. Consistent interactions are at the core of a relational journey that builds a healthy bond. There is a metaphor regarding relationship building in an ancient book that states, "iron sharpens iron." Relationships like strong iron can bring out and forge our best selves.

People who influenced my life have helped me find my voice to speak with relevance into the lives of others with a loving grace that empowers. Many of my relational experiences mirror the maxim "iron sharpens iron." These relationships were not all characterized by tranquil encounters. There were tough-love confrontations that caused friction as well.

Relational dynamics create an environment that will either terminate or enhance relationships. The reward for consistency in a relational journey of tough-love friction produces teachable moments for growth. Developing a diversity program is like an ongoing relational journey that include both harmonious and difficult experiences which lead to the formation of an ID Transformational organization.

Consistency Component

My consistency component for the Sustainability Building Block refers to building an ID Transformation culture not as a destination but rather as a journey. When leaders focus on resolving the diversity disparity in their organizations with little effort towards building a culture, their programs become a short-term destination. It takes less time to hire individuals from different backgrounds than to develop an organizational culture of belonging that retains those new hires. Without taking the time and consistency to build an inclusive culture, organizations will not create an environment that fully embraces diversity, equity, and inclusion.

Rather than band-aid approaches, leaders need to model and develop a behavioral pattern of consistency that seeks permanent solutions for diversity and equity disparities. Instead of deploying a destination mentality to fix an immediate problem, my consistency component suggests a journey approach of consistent action that creates inclusive mindsets capable of embracing diversity.

Building a culture of belonging has to involve more than simply focusing on the lack of a diverse workforce. A short-term fix will not produce a permanent solution for a historical problem. Inequities and biases did not occur overnight; therefore, a quick fix will not resolve a situation that requires a consistent approach for renewal.

The consistency component is the exact opposite of the usual business approach that tries to respond to rapidly shifting marketplace demands. The dynamics in creating a diversity program cannot use the same fast turnaround approach required when providing goods and services. A diversity program involves consistency for nurturing and developing human relationships, which a rapid method is inefficient. Building an organizational culture of *interconnected individuals leading to a palpable sense of belonging* is a collaborative effort requiring slow, steady, and patient consistency.

Society is approaching the fourth Industrial Revolution (the first three being steam engine, electrical, and digital) based upon the "internet of things" and cyber-biological systems. If diversity programs don't become ID Transformational, they will be irrelevant within an industrial revolution paradigm shift.

Since most research shows that diversity programs are not producing the intended outcomes, it is a good indication that these programs won't survive as we enter the next societal shift. That's why we need the consistency component for building block five as a means for diversity workers to develop a culture that is not a fast-track approach that will not sustain social paradigm shifts.

Diversity programs must become more innovative to create relevant and sustainable practices. Diversity programs must be models of consistency involving critical thinking, creativity, and problem solving to respond to the organizational challenges and changing social trends. Thus, the consistency component for building block five is vital when developing a sustainable diversity program in the mist of continuous social paradigm shifts.

CRITICAL-THINKING EXERCISE

Developing an ID Transformational program is a long-term process of consistency. The following steps outline my consistent approach as a Diversity and Inclusion Program Manager toward creating an ID Transformation program:

1. The first step is to research the information about diversity within other organizations.
2. Take note of their best practices for diversity and inclusion from your research.
3. Sift through the information to find the golden nuggets on diversity and inclusion that are relevant for your organization.
4. Then take time to reflect on your research and how you can incorporate the best practices you've found.
5. Think about your current organizational culture and about how it could become an ideal culture for belonging.
6. Connect the research to your organization and evaluate the similarities and differences.
7. Think about new best practices from your research and how they can apply to your organization.
8. Think about best practices you can create specifically for your organization.
9. Do more research and subscribe to articles and journals on diversity and inclusion best practices and challenges.

10. Do research on organizational change and compare it to the adaptive change required for diversity within your organization.

11. Think about how to help your organization lay the building blocks to guide the development of an ID Transformation program.

Note: All steps are recurring processes. Keep in mind that creating a diversity program is like planting a flower garden. It's a consistent process of planting, fertilizing, pruning, and weeding.

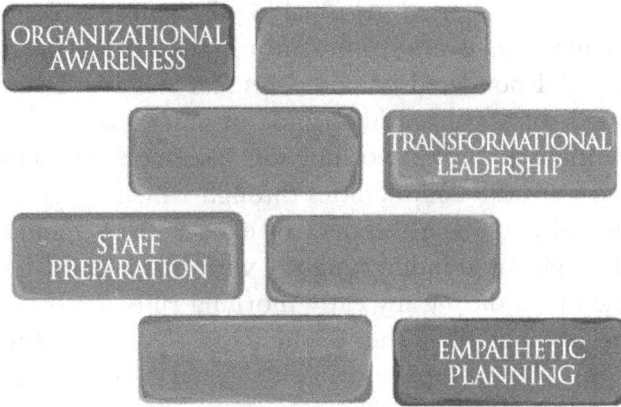

SUSTAINABILITY

ORGANIZATIONAL
AWARENESS

TRANSFORMATIONAL
LEADERSHIP

STAFF
PREPARATION

EMPATHETIC
PLANNING

CHAPTER 12

REFLECTION

"It's on the strength of observation and reflection that one finds a way. So, we must dig and delve unceasingly." – Claude Monet

My Practitioner's Lens

The pandemic was a time of reflection for me. Mentally, I sought a quiet place amid the voices of fear, uncertainty, political unrest, espoused values disguised as truth, tribalism, and mistrust. Mornings are a quiet time when I seek a peaceful environment from distracting voices of social dialog. These times of peaceful and quiet reflection are always mentally stimulating.

I am also an early morning jogger because of the calm and quiet atmosphere before the hustle and bustle of the day begins. This time has always served as my meditation period. Occasionally during my jogging and meditation, the ah-ha moments of clarity penetrate my mind. At the beginning of COVID-19, I experienced an unusual and disturbing situation during my morning jog at the time of the mandated restrictions.

As I started my usual jog through several communities, there was an overwhelming fear in the atmosphere like a heavy cloud. I pondered whether this fear was within me and why, but I soon realized it was not an inner fear but external, like running through a morning fog. It seemed to be a fear resonating from the communities through which I jogged. As I continued jogging, a moment of extraordinary tranquility broke through my mindful unrest. I wish that type of moment was the norm during my early morning runs. Unfortunately, they are rare, but when they occur, it's an ah-ha moment of clarity.

That moment of clarity helped me realize there was also a positive side to COVID-19. It provided me a season which I find mentally rejuvenating as described by Christine Caine: "Sometimes when you're in a dark place you think you've been buried, but actually you've been planted." I decided to view the duration of COVID-19 as my time of being a buried seed that dies in order to enter a transformational cycle of growth and productivity. My ah-ha moment then posed a question: Would I stagnate during COVID-19, or would I use it as a season of growth and insight? Writing this book is one of three sustainable commitments I made to myself during that time.

Reflection Component

You may wonder about the significance of referring to my ah-ha experience that I am labeling reflection. Reflections are significant thoughts that come from life shaping-experiences. Creating time for reflection can provide clarity from situations of complexity and uncertainty. Developing a diversity program to develop organizational harmony can be perplexing and overwhelming. When creating a new environment, DI leaders and staff must go beyond research and learning theories. Digging beneath the surface of espoused values, best practices, and challenges is essential to gain a broader perspective. Reflection provides avenues to explore beyond traditional beliefs to uncover novel ideas.

You may be thinking, "How can reflection provide new insights for DI workers?" The reflection component for the Sustainability Building Block is comprised of three key concepts that provide the answer: passion, authenticity, and knowledge. Without these three concepts, reflection produces superficial thoughts that lack the power needed for ID Transformation.

- *Passion* is the strong feeling or desire necessary to build a diversity program that guides an organization to its fullest potential. When people are passionate about creating a culture of belonging, their efforts involve more than a check box mentality. Diversity programs will go much farther when initiatives are more than doing the right thing. Implementing initiatives should come from a heart of dedication and resolve to create an environment that promotes and celebrates all individuals.

- *Authenticity* is who you are and what you do that are in line with your values and beliefs. It is also a growth process that leads to your fullest potential. DI workers need to lead from the inside out—becoming their best selves and inspiring others to become the same. Diversity programs can be transformative catalysts in organizations that draw their energy from workers' capacity to willingly influence, motivate, stimulate, and consider all individuals and people groups.

- *Knowledge* is information that is understood and acquired from experience and education. It is essential to understand the specific subject matter of any area of work. Life experiences and education shape a worker's worldview; thus, the

broader their worldview, the more impact they
will have on developing a sustainable program
that advances an organization.

There is a common thread that runs between passion,
authenticity, and knowledge. They all reside within an individual and each one empowers reflection. Passion, authenticity, and knowledge are facets of self-awareness which reflection
taps into, thus enabling imagination and birthing innovation.
This concept is the basis that provides context for my *reflection
component.*

When leaders and staff are intentional while developing a synergistic diversity program, reflection helps create *a
palpable sense of belonging that increases human and organizational capacity for progressive innovation.* Self-awareness comprised
of passion, authenticity, and knowledge is vital for reflective
moments that in turn foster critical thinking, creativity, and
problem-solving.

Also, it is worth mentioning that a lack of self-awareness limits reflection results. Thus, when DI workers are passionate about creating a culture of belonging, embrace their

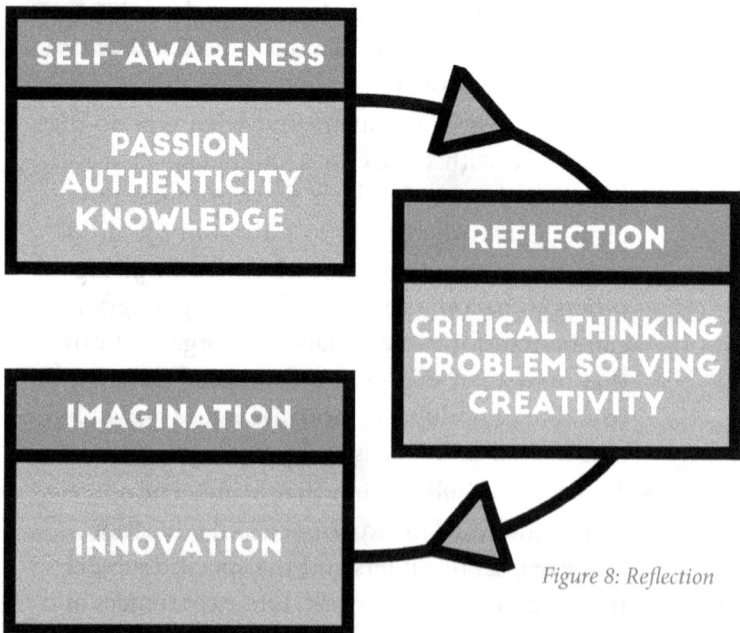

SELF-AWARENESS

PASSION
AUTHENTICITY
KNOWLEDGE

REFLECTION

CRITICAL THINKING
PROBLEM SOLVING
CREATIVITY

IMAGINATION

INNOVATION

Figure 8: Reflection

authentic selves, and are committed to increasing knowledge through new learning experiences, they will benefit from being self-aware during reflective moments, as seen in Figure 8.

Einstein famously said: "Logic will get you from A to Z; imagination will get you everywhere." Reflection opens the mind to that much-needed imagination. Reflection periods also provide a broader perspective that goes beyond experiences and education. Reflection is nurtured by passion, authenticity, and knowledge, thus birthing innovation.

DI workers need to take time and step away from their day-to-day tasks of developing programs so they can reflect. The reflection is where meaningful ah-ha moments can occur. Leaders can miss the small or big picture situations that will make a significant difference in developing a program.

Like my reflection time during early morning jogs, every DI worker can find their best quiet time and place for reflection—going for a walk, sitting in a park, bike riding, etc. Many concepts for this chapter's reflection component and other building block components for ID Transformation were ideas generated from my reflection during a morning jog. An organizational diversity program can benefit from leaders and staff creating an environment for reflection that can answer complex questions and provide answers to situations never imagined. Time in reflection can allow DI workers to focus within and examine outward trends and realities to increase self-transformation, which will enhance organizational capacity for ID Transformation.

CRITICAL-THINKING EXERCISE

I have introduced practical components for building blocks to guide the development and implement of an ID Transformation program. To develop such a program, the right questions must be asked to create best practices for your unique institutional culture. I have generated the following questions for you to ponder during your reflection moments. Hopefully, these questions will stimulate more questions that lead to creative answers as you seek to develop innovative initiatives:

1. How do you define diversity, equity, and inclusion?

2. How have your life-shaping experiences formed your definition of diversity, equity, and inclusion?

3. How has your involvement or lack of participation in diverse environments affected your worldview?

4. What are some of your adaptive challenges with diversity and how are they affecting your organization?

5. What is the status of diversity, equity, and inclusion in your organization?

6. What steps has your organization taken to advance diversity and inclusion practices?

7. What do you foresee as adaptive challenges to achieving diversity within your organization?

8. How can you address the adaptive challenges

you envision in your organization that are within your influence?

9. What are the known strengths, weaknesses, opportunities, and threats in your organization relative to diversity?

10. In what ways can you model and encourage diversity and inclusion within your organization to influence others in meaningful ways?

Reflecting and asking the right questions are the starting point for developing your diversity program. What are some questions that are not on the above list?

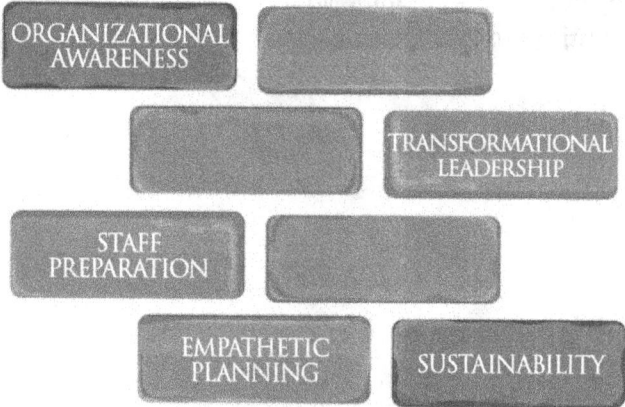

CHAPTER 13

DESTINATION—
ID TRANSFORMATION

*"If we don't change direction soon, we'll end up where
we're going."* – Irwin Corey

Additional Building Block

I have described five building blocks for implementing an ID Transformation program: organizational awareness,

transformational leadership, staff preparation, empathetic planning, and sustainability. When thinking about individuals who show up to work daily and give their best service to organizations that underappreciate, undervalue, and never champion them, I would suggest a sixth *Building Block: Ownership.* This Building Block consists of *metanoia* and *rectification components.*

To be fully committed to creating a culture of belonging, I give the same advice to institutions my parents gave me as an adolescent: when participating in a misdeed, take *ownership* by acknowledging the wrong and rectifying actions. Therefore, when creating diversity programs, remember the Ownership Building Block. Diversity workers should also address any role they have had, whether intentional or unintentional, in limiting DEI in their organization. Metanoia is a Greek word meaning "to change one's mind or purpose." Thus, the *metanoia component represents a change of heart towards practices that do not support a wholesome environment for all staff.*

This action will also help leaders avoid using empty words of appreciation and inactions to exclude, neutralize, or subjugate staff. Furthermore, the *rectification component implements policies and procedures that prevent staff infractions and thus impede* the creation of an ID Transformational culture. What's more, to ensure organizational well-being, accountability safeguards should be established.

As a Diversity and Inclusion Program Manager, I have had a lifetime *passion* for serving and embracing diverse people groups; *authenticity* to develop a heart of grace enabling me to consider the needs of others; and a thirst for *knowledge* that fueled my lifelong learning that empowered my worldview to understand myself and others.

Hopefully, you received helpful insight and resources from my book that stimulate your thinking and guide a conversation that will develop a diversity program unique to your organization. If you ask, "Where do I start the journey toward ID transformation?", you have asked an important question. Whatever your position as a leader or follower, the journey starts with *you.* Your ID for transformation is essential—knowing who you are will help get you started and influence others on the journey towards ID Transformation.

In chapter six, I wrote about the importance of knowing your *position* from life-shaping experiences before creating an action plan for change (*disposition*). Your journey toward ID Transformation must start by first understanding your purpose or discovering your purpose and professional mission. This life aspect is similar to a traveler knowing their location before getting directions to a desired destination.

Perhaps this leads to a second question: "What do purpose and professional mission have to do with creating a diversity program?" I explained earlier in chapter seven how my purpose and professional mission were consistent with my serving in a new position as a Diversity and Inclusion Program Manager. The same relates to your endeavor as a diversity worker. Without understanding yourself and how you connect with diversity work, you will not reach the intended destination of creating *relationally-interconnected individuals who create a palpable sense of belonging that increases human and organizational capacity for progressive innovation.*

Reaching The Destination

Your life's purpose and professional mission represent the vehicle that gets you to the destination of ID Transformation. The directions and fuel are needed to ignite any vehicle to the desired destination. Lacking a roadmap and energy for ID Transformation produces empty words that don't reflect actions. As my uncle would verbalize, "What you do speaks so loud, I can't hear what you say." After reading this book, I hope your journey towards ID Transformation becomes more than rhetoric but actions in sync with your purpose and professional mission.

Figure 9 puts into context the process needed to reach your diversity program's goals relative to vehicle, directions, and fuel. The starting point in the figure is your purpose and professional mission, which is the vehicle that shapes who you are. If you are unaware of your purpose and professional mission, you need to find resources that help you discover your purpose. Numerous online resources and workshops facilitate discovering your purpose. Once your purpose and professional mission are known, this is the vehicle that will determine if you have or need to develop the qualities required for diversity work.

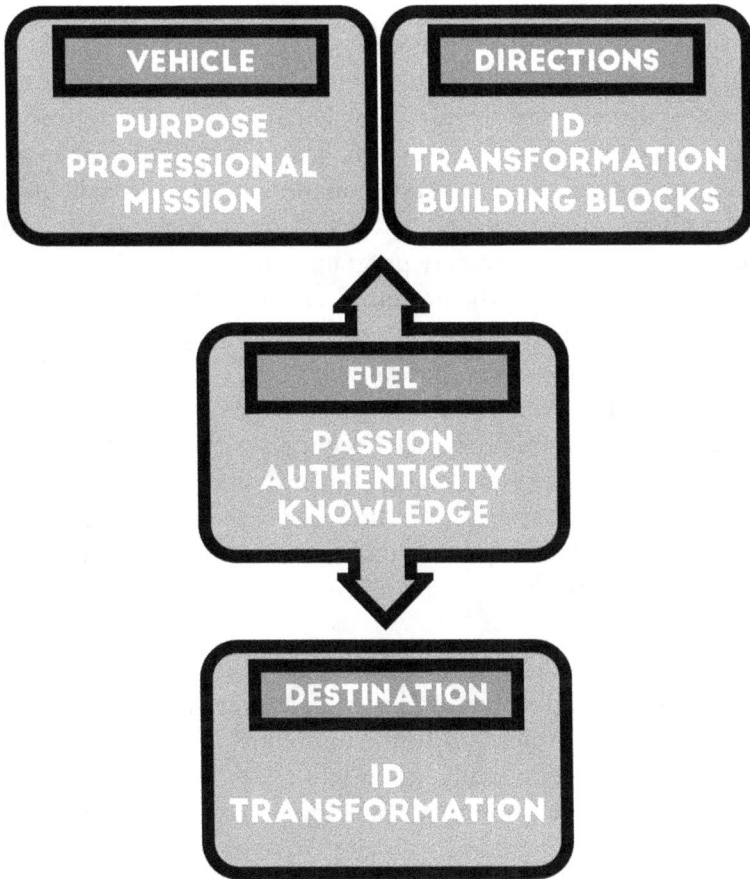

Figure 9: Destination – ID Transformation

Second, directions are vital in guiding to a destination. Thus, the building blocks serve as your guide in creating a culture of ID Transformation. The Building Blocks Organizational Awareness, Transformational Leadership, Staff Preparation, Empathetic Planning, Sustainability, and Ownership, along with their foundation of Adaptive Challenge and Vision are all essential for ID Transformation. As you have read, each building block consist of components for you to utilize in your organization to develop a relevant and sustaining diversity program. Avoid using the building blocks only as espoused values (mottos and statements) during your journey. Incorporating the building blocks into your underlying assumption (actions and daily practices) that sync with espoused values will produce evidence of ID Transformation.

Third, the fuel ignites your purpose and professional mission for diversity work. A vehicle has a purpose but cannot function without power. The same is true when your purpose and professional mission lack the energy for action; it will limit your ability to achieve your program's mission. As leaders and participants build a diversity program, it takes effort. In chapter twelve, I write about the power of reflection. The energy I express in the chapter will ignite your vehicle (purpose and professional mission) that will move you in the direction (building blocks) needed to reach your organizational ID Transformation destination. Without the fuel from passion, authenticity, and knowledge, you will only be going through the motions getting nowhere or espousing values that are not in sync with your actions. Passion, authenticity, and knowledge referred to in chapter twelve will galvanize your journey towards ID Transformation.

- *Passion* is the strong feeling or desire necessary to build a diversity program that guides an organization to its fullest potential. Your efforts go beyond words when you are *passionate* about creating a culture of belonging. Implementing diversity initiatives should come from a heart of dedication to creating an environment that promotes and celebrates all individuals.
- Authenticity is who you are and what you do that are in line with your values and beliefs. It is also a growth process that leads to your fullest potential. As a DI worker you need to lead from the inside out—becoming your best selves and inspiring others to become the same. Diversity programs can be transformative catalysts in organizations that draw their energy from workers' capacity to willingly influence, motivate, stimulate, and consider all individuals and people groups.
- *Knowledge* is information that is understood and acquired from experience and education.

Understanding the subject matter of DEI is essential in creating a diversity program. Your life and education experiences will shape your worldview. Thus, the broader your worldview, the more impact you will have on developing a sustainable program that advances an organization.

A diversity worker's passion for unity, authenticity for truthfulness that directs, and lifelong educational learning are essential in utilizing the building blocks effectively to create your diversity program. Your interest in reading this book and being equipped for the journey towards ID Transformation is commendable. I wish you the best in your desire and efforts to become your best self so you can participate in the development of a sense of belonging within your organization that embraces and celebrates a diverse community.

Hopefully, my building blocks for ID Transformation and other DEI resources will provide value for your diversity program and guide you in modeling the way for ID Transformation that creates *relationally-interconnected individuals who create a palpable sense of belonging that increases human and organizational capacity for progressive innovation.*

CONCLUSION

"Progress is impossible without change, and those who
cannot change their minds cannot change anything."
– George Bernard Shaw

Prepare For Change

The twenty-first-century diversity phenomenon is in
its infancy in many organizations given the United States'
historical roots of racial and gender biases entangled in institutional norms. As I researched the matters surrounding
diversity, much of the rhetoric sounded the same, giving
little practical methodology for how to develop a relevant
and sustainable diversity program. Thus, I created the five ID
Transformational Building Blocks as a practical guide to help
you develop a viable diversity program. Two components define each building block. Let's take a moment to review my
building blocks:

- **Building Block One: Organizational
  Awareness** consists of culture and
  accountability components. The culture
  component is comprised of *artifacts* (the
  structure of a workplace), *espoused values*
  (what is said and written, such as mottos and
  mission), and *underlying assumptions* (how staff
  interact with each other and constituents)
  within an organization. Knowing how these
  cultural elements are in sync or not is critical
  before developing a diversity program. The
  accountability component is a mechanism for

evaluating, improving, and assessing the evidence of a culture of ID Transformation.

- **Building Block Two: Transformational Leadership** consists of influence and worldview components. The influence component is the positive effect of a transformational leader in developing an ID Transformational culture. This leadership style leads staff through *idealized influence, inspirational motivation, intellectual stimulation,* and *individualized consideration.* The *worldview component* is a process to guide managers and supervisors to adjust or broaden their worldview through *position* (assessing current life-shaping position), disposition (making necessary adjustments or changes for growth mindset), and *reposition* (achieving a broader understanding of self and others).

- **Building Block Three: Staff Preparation** contains purpose and advancement components. The purpose component is the process of discovering your life›s purpose. Knowing your purpose is essential in impacting your professional mission and organizational progress. The advancement component is an accountability process to assist you in a continuous and personalized learning and development plan that advances your professional mission and shows how it aligns with the organizational mission.

- **Building Block Four: Empathetic Planning** consists of strategy and collaboration components. This component involves organizational action, such as mission, values, policy, buy-in, resources, and creativity that guide your diversity program. These actions are leadership-driven with staff involvement through empathetic planning that considers and celebrates diverse mindsets and backgrounds. All organizational activities should align with the mission, avoiding any deficiencies affecting efficient outcomes within the diversity program. The collaboration component is a shared partnership process among leaders and staff to oversee administration and staff engagement for a diversity program.

- **Building Block Five: Sustainability** emanates from consistent and reflective practices. The consistency component creates a culture of ID Transformation that is not a short-term fix for a problem but a long-term process that establishes a new environment of belonging. The reflection component combines one's passion, authenticity, and knowledge to create a sustainable ID Transformation diversity program through critical thinking, creativity, and problem-solving.

- **Building Block Six: Ownership** consists of the metanoia and rectification components. The *metanoia component represents a change of heart regarding practices that do not support a wholesome environment for all staff. This action helps* leaders avoid using empty words of appreciation and inactions while excluding, neutralizing, or subjugating staff. The *rectification component implements policies and procedures that prevent staff infractions that impede* achieving an ID Transformational culture. What's more, to ensure organizational well-being, accountability safeguards should also be established.

As a practitioner of institutional development, before I create learning and development initiatives, my first approach is to understand the learners' needs for improvement and the institutional objectives for staff advancement. I used this same training approach when developing my *Building Blocks for ID Transformation that represent interconnected-individuals producing a palpable sense of belonging that increases human and organizational capacity for progressive innovation.* My initial attempt to understand an audience's learning needs is the prerequisite for developing training that will enhance learning outcomes that are relevant and sustainable.

I would conclude that most organizational diversity programs fail stemming from an eagerness to incorporate hiring practices to correct the disparity of workplace diversity without first doing the hard work of culture change. Before organizations can initiate plans to diversify, they must first evaluate their culture's strengths and weaknesses where diversity is concerned. A good foundation for developing an organizational vision for diversity includes the following principles: know, develop, and prepare.

- To *know* the current culture and have a good understanding of the ideal culture that will foster belonging; organizations need to know where they are and where they want to be.

- To *develop* a learning and development environment that enhances professional efficacy while also broadening an individual's worldview that will advance human and organizational capacity; organizations must be committed to transformation.

- To *prepare* leaders and staff for the adaptive challenges associated with organizational change; organizations need to identify and minimize barriers that make change difficult.

Before an individual embarks upon a journey, not only is the destination essential but *knowing* the current location and directions are equally crucial. The same is true when an organization plans to implement diversity as part of its mission and vision. Most organizations have deep historical roots that manifest in their structure and culture. It is essential to *know* their traditions that can hinder or support a vision for diversity.

To *develop* is to incorporate diversity and inclusion training into the organizational learning and development program. Learning platforms will help create an environment that increases workplace proficiency while also advancing organizational innovation. Training programs will broaden an individual's worldview, providing a deeper awareness of self and others and increasing cultural respect and collaboration.

To *prepare* is to guide leaders and staff through the adaptive change of diversity. Organizational change can be difficult for leaders and staff to embrace because they are not ready for a cultural paradigm shift. When diversity practices have not been part of the organizational culture, anxieties emerge when creating a culture of inclusion. Preparation should be part of any learning and development program, steps that will guide individuals through the change processes that affect both the organization and the individual. Learning and development will also provide resources that support awareness and achieve the intended change.

Diversity is becoming more necessary for organizational wellbeing, but the adaptive change to bring it about is not given much thought when implementing diversity practices. The workplace shift to create this paradigm requires leadership and staff not only to develop their hard skills but also their soft ones. The soft skills can increase interpersonal engagement as new challenges from a diverse and inclusive environment arise. Because of the adaptive challenges caused by diversity efforts, both leaders and staff need to engage in learning and personal development that will change hearts and increase job proficiency as the workplace evolves.

Researchers suggest that the shaping of an individual's personality is complete around eight years of age. Given the development of individuals' worldviews also occurs during their early years, most individuals do not voluntarily seek change. Change is difficult, and many individuals struggle with it. Therefore, a significant attribute of adaptive leadership is the ability to lead staff through an ever-changing environment.

Kegan Lahey (2001) stated that individuals deal with adaptive challenges based on mindsets shaped by their worldviews. Leaders must be aware of staff attitudes that hinder change, such as fears in learning new skills and assignments. When knowing staff's fears toward change, leaders can provide appropriate learning and development that guide and empower staff for change.

As issues arise that impede change, adaptive leadership must help staff seek continuous learning and development to meet the workplace changes initiated by diversity. Trust and respect are the first key principles for leaders to establish with staff. When staff trust and respect their leaders, they will be more likely to value the importance of growing with their organization.

Kevin Cashman (2008) argues that an effective leader leads by example from the inside out, first developing one's best self. As leaders lead by example, they can then empower staff to increase their professional proficiency. Staff who are committed to organizational development experience positive outcomes within their workplace environment. As staff acquire professional efficacy that contributes to the institutional mission, they then share in the adventures of institutional advancement.

There is a need to redefine diversity programs in a much broader context than I have heretofore witnessed in many institutions. Many organizations have implemented diversity and inclusion programs to provide advancement opportunities, but they lack the intended outcomes. ID can be disguised as forward-thinking when there are no attempts to dismantle the historical roots of inequities. To remedy this, I developed the building blocks to help leaders and staff build an ID Transformation program unique to their organizations. The building blocks do not have rigid or restrictive components that lack flexibility. They establish a starting place and foundation to create and develop an ID Transformation program.

We tend to categorize and compartmentalize things and people into neat packages and bundles that create boundaries and barriers to growth. Because of this, often seek to condense or reduce the components of our world into neat, easy-to-explain categories. Our universe is vastly diverse and functions in unity with an orderly consistency but is ever-changing and expanding.

When individuals recognize the transforming power in the universe and pattern diversity programs upon similar transformational principles, we will witness a launching pad for discovering untapped organizational potential. Is this why haven't we grasped the true essence of inclusion and diversity? Perhaps this is why most diversity programs are failing or not gaining the momentum to flourish?

To see possibilities in the true reality of diversity, we must go beyond the context of celebrating diverse people groups without understanding individuals in their context. As citizens of a constantly changing universe, we are continuously developing and growing. So, how can I or anyone else be contextualized by only a name or people group? People are transitional and transformational beings; whatever people group they identify with becomes more than an ethnic label. When organizations broaden their worldview where people groups are concerned, the context of diversity becomes robust. Organizations have yet to discover the hidden potential of an ever-progressive diversity that is revolutionary and transforms inclusion from assimilating, or simply belonging, to interdependency.

When leaders lead from their personal biases and conform to institutional systems of racial, gender, and other mental/physical biases, workplaces become like a brick wall blocking growth. For ID Transformation to go beyond the walls of inequalities, leadership and staff development programs must transform hearts that can tear down organizational walls and lead to areas of tangible inclusion.

I think of Plato's *Allegory of the Cave* when leaders in organizations chain their staff to the walls of biases and microaggressions. In the *Allegory of the Cave*, Socrates describes prisoners chained to a cave wall with their backs to the cave opening. When people or animals outside of the cave passed by the cave, the prisoners could only see shadows on the cave walls. The shadows became the prisoner's reality of people and animal images. When one of the prisoners was released from his chains and went outside, he experienced the wonders of actual reality for the first time.

There is more to this allegory, but my point referencing it here is that barriers are inevitable when leaders and staff biases—shadows of reality—prevent them from seeing the beauty and power that ID Transformation brings to the workplace. As a practitioner and educator, I encourage you to use my Building Blocks for ID Transformation to understand your culture, leadership development, and preparing staff for change relative to twenty-first-century diversity realities.

An ID Transformational culture is synergetic. It is essential for diversity workers to research and sift through all the overwhelming information for gold nuggets that will best serve their organizations. It is crucial that institutional vision for diversity include organizational awareness, transformational leadership, and staff preparation, and then plan with empathy and sustainability in mind. This book provides a practical and big-picture approach that provides fundamental guidance for building ID Transformation that goes beyond the rhetoric to transform workplaces into synergistic and evolving cultures.

If you have questions or want to further discuss the Building Blocks, I am available for consultations, presentations, and workshops that will enhance your journey toward ID Transformation. Best wishes on your journey!

EPILOGUE

"What you do speaks so loud, I can't hear what you say."
– My uncle's words of wisdom

Beyond The Rhetoric

Although the pandemic presented numerous challenges as we adapted to a new norm of living, it also provided opportunities for reflection and critical thinking. I have reflected long and hard about my experiences as both a practitioner and adjunct faculty in higher education, sometimes on those early morning jogs I mentioned earlier. I have grown and continue to grow because of professional experiences that have given me an appreciation for diversity and lifelong learning. The numerous individuals who benefited from my leadership and teaching contributions have also helped me expand my worldview.

Borrowing the words of Dr. Martin Luther King Jr., my life mission is to "develop a heart full of grace and a soul generated by love" that will enrich and empower the lives of others through my passion for teaching and transformational leadership. I desire that leaders and staff find my building blocks and information in this book helpful as they develop an effective strategic plan to implement a significant diversity program unique to their organization. My building blocks will serve to develop a tangible ID Transformation program. My practitioner experience in institutional development, diversity research, and critical thinking toward organizational transformation have shaped this practical approach to guide the emergence of ID Transformation beyond the rhetoric.

Diversity is an important response to societal cries for

social justice as institutions re-examine their inclusion practices. To meet the adaptive challenge of diversity in institutions,
leaders and staff must look inward to resolve biases that stem
from indoctrination and falsehoods disguised as truth before
workplace transformation can occur. It is easy to treat the
symptoms of inequity by adjusting demographic measurements
rather than doing the hard work of healing the root causes of
the inequity symptoms. Diversity programs have to become
more than a band-aid treatment for inequities but should rather
seek to address the root causes of historical bias that has resulted
in contemporary institutional exclusion.

In 2020, our nation witnessed the gruesome murder of
Mr. George Floyd at the hands of law officers who had no re-
gard for Mr. Floyd's humanity. Many individuals were outraged
by Mr. Floyd's murder which prompted a national outcry for
social justice. This national tragedy, reinforced by similar viola-
tions, forced institutions to open their eyes to the social injustices prevalent in our institutions. The institutions with which I
am affiliated have added their voices to the public cries for social justice in America. I listened to numerous virtual platforms
of organizations expressing both their discontent with the status quo and also their commitment to more actively fighting
against social injustices occurring in their communities.

I was bewildered when hearing these institutional ex-
pressions of dissatisfaction with the status quo and they gave me
pause. My question was: Do you (institutions) see individuals
who continue to feel invisible and disenfranchised within your
own institutions? Many institutions seemed to see injustices in
their local and national systems but could not see the transgres-
sions within their own workplace environments.

Another question I would also like to ask institutions
that desire to implement diversity programs is, "Can you press
beyond the smiles of the subjugated staff and see their pain?"
Despite their pain, they continue to advance the organizational
mission while still experience subjective assessments and out-
dated performance appraisals that cannot discover hidden talents, thus never being championed for their potential.

I hope my building blocks will serve as a lighthouse

that provides clarity on your ID Transformational journey as you influence and motivate others in a collective effort to build an environment of belonging. My intent for this book is to serve as a blueprint for diversity that will guide leaders and staff to build an organizational culture of inclusion and equity that is relevant and sustaining. Diversity programs will never go beyond the rhetoric of DEI ideologies if inequities and biases are hidden or blurry. Hopefully, you connect with my building blocks that will stimulate and inspire your actions, influencing others to grow and collaborate in ID Transformational building. Thus, "What you do speaks so loud, I can't hear what you say."

APPENDIX

Chapter Two: Vision is part of my book's Foundation for ID Transformation. In that chapter, I explained the importance for organizations to have clear, concise, and short- and long-term directives that achieve significant outcomes for their organizational diversity program. In the charter section of the chapter, I referred to *Appendix: Guide for Organizational Inclusion and Diversity (ID) Charter.*

The Table 2 is a guide to assist you in writing your diversity program's charter. Also, when drafting a charter, think about the following:

1. *What is a charter?*
   - A document of your intended goals for a diversity program.
2. Steps to writing a charter:
   - Choose a name for your diversity program.
   - Draft the mission for your diversity program.
   - Outline team participants and define their responsibilities.
   - Develop policies and procedures that align with DEI.
   - Determine short and long-term objectives.
   - Create an action plan in order to accomplish objectives.
   - Assess resources needed.
   - Set up a timeline for accomplishments.
   - Create metrics to evaluate the success or failure of goals.

TABLE 2: GUIDE FOR ORGANIZATIONAL INCLUSION AND DIVERSITY (ID) CHARTER

MISSION

An ID mission conveys a commitment to build a welcoming organization where its members have a sense of belonging. Writing the statement should be a group initiative—select a committee consisting of leaders and staff from different professional and personal backgrounds. Keep the following in mind when drafting an ID mission:

1. Clearly written
2. Inclusive language
3. Diverse people groups
4. ID behavioral practices
5. ID mission aligns with the organization-at-large mission

Example of an ID mission: Our organization is committed to cultivating a sense of belonging that embraces new ways of thinking through valuing opinions, respecting differences, while also encouraging personal and professional development.

WORKING GROUP

A working group is a team with a passion for working collaboratively to create a sense of belonging within an ID Transformational organization. The group consists of representatives from different backgrounds throughout the organization. The working group intends to establish staff engagement, development, and administrative procedures that promote an inclusive culture that embraces diversity while increasing innovation within the workplace. Keep in mind: Engagement from leadership at all levels is a critical component to achieving successful outcomes toward establishing a culture of belonging by the following:

1. Create trust and respect.

2. Articulate the vision.

3. Model the way.

POLICY

An ID policy statement is a written agreement so the people involved will avoid discriminatory actions and establish equitable decisions regarding staff. The policy should clearly state the aim to eliminate unfair systemic barriers that excludes marginalized people.

When drafting an ID policy, keep in mind equitable decision-making practices in the following areas:

1. Recruitment and hiring

2. Promotion

3. Compensation

4. Employee development

An example of an ID policy is as follows: All decisions safeguard and contribute to the well-being of the following: race, religious beliefs, color, gender, sexual orientation, marital status, physical and mental disability, age, ancestry, and place of origin.

PRACTICES

A statement for ID practices communicates best practices that confirm a sense of belonging in an innovative workplace, such as fairness, collaboration, and growth opportunities. It will also emphasize the importance of celebrating people by respecting and appreciating what makes them different.

Here are some examples of best practices:

1. Compliance with human rights legislation.

2. Fair and equitable treatment that applies to all aspects of employment.

3. Management assurance that all policies, practices, and procedures do not permit intentional or unintentional discrimination.

4. Management mandates that their workforce reflects the communities they serve.

5. Creating a more inclusive workplace where staff feels welcomed and motivated.

6. Developing an environment in which staff work productively because of their differences.

OBJECTIVES

The objectives provide means for developing, implementing, and achieving the mission.

Consider the following ID initiatives when drafting an approach for cultivating a sense of belonging:

1. Equitable opportunities for all staff

2. Embracing collaboration among staff

3. Initiating team-building in the workplace

4. Targeting marginalized people groups

5. Learning and development programs

Example of objectives:

1. Develop administrative efforts to oversee the development and implementation initiatives for building a welcoming workplace experience.

2. Create employee resource groups for engagement, education, and celebratory activities.

3. Implement communication platforms to provide information and advertisements regarding ID events.

4. Participate with diversity networks to learn and share best practices and challenges.

ACTION PLAN

An action plan for an ID program is a framework to guide strategic efforts to build a welcoming workplace experience through behavioral practices that break down intentional and unintentional barriers of biases and discrimination. The action plan provides short and long-terms goals for achieving an ID Transformational culture.

Things to consider when establishing an action plan:

1. Meaningful initiatives unique to an organization

2. Pinpoint areas of concern

3. Determine the current cultural climate

4. Elements of an ideal welcoming workplace

5. Starting point for building a welcoming culture

6. Metrics for evaluation, improvement, and assessment

Example of metrics:

Answers the following questions:

1. What *resources* are needed?

2. How are we going to be held *responsible?*

3. How are we going to measure our *improvement?*

4. By what *date* do we want to reach our goal?

5. How will we *assess* the results of our outcome?

6. What are your *key performance indicators* (tangible objectives)?

Examples of goals:

Communications and staff engagement are vital components for establishing a belonging workplace. The following initiatives provide examples of goals for staff interactions that build a welcoming workplace experience.

1. *Communications:* The goal is to provide various communication platforms to help staff stay informed with diversity, equity, and inclusion best practices that promote and create a sense of belonging. The methods for messaging are as follows:

- Monthly newsletter announcements to inform, inspire, and challenge.
- Weekly or bi-weekly email messages to inform, inspire, and challenge.
- Online (Microsoft Teams, Zoom, etc.) question-and-answer sessions with staff.

2. *Staff engagement:* The goal is to build a platform that allows staff to communicate and regularly interact for social activities, professional development, and insightful dialogue through the channels of:

- *Engagement:* Onboarding, Employee Resource Groups (ERG), Learning and Development Resources.
- *Open forum:* Discussion Groups.
- *Networking:* Participation in diversity, equity, and inclusion groups within and outside the organization.

3. *Staff climate survey:* This is a good starting point to evaluate the workplace environment. Staff hard and soft skills contribute to the successful outcomes of the organizational mission in maintaining relevant and sustainable resources and services. Therefore, to obtain an accurate assessment of staff and leadership impact upon the organization's mission, an annual staff climate survey can be used to assess the following categories: demographics, workplace experience, and leadership support. This survey would serve as an evaluation process to measure the current effectiveness and possible improvement needs for framing the mission and best practices for diversity, equity, and inclusion.

- Mission statement: revise the organizational mission statement to incorporate the information revealed from survey data. The revised mission will reflect input from the organization at large.

4. *Workplace experience survey:* A working group would consist of members from the leadership team and staff to oversee the effectiveness of procedures to help evaluate the workplace experience. A tool and method should be implemented to assess the workplace experience from a staff perspective.

Note: The climate and workplace experience survey's development can be created by a capable in-house team, office of human resources, or an external company that can provide survey services and resources.

REFERENCES

Caine, Christine. (2022). Pinterest. *Pinterest.com: https://www.pinterest. com/pin/371687775475380180/*

Cashman, K. (2008). Leadership from the inside out: Becoming a leader for life (2nd ed.). San Francisco: Berrett-Koehler.

Covey, Stephen R., (1989). *The Seven Habits of Highly Effective People.* New York, NY: Simon & Schuster Publishers.

Einstein, Albert. (2022). Albert Einstein Quotes. *BrainyQuote. com:* https://www.brainyquote.com/quotes/albert_einstein_ 121643

Einstein, Albert. (2022). Pinterest. *Pinterest.com: https://www.pinterest. com/pin/423690277427812944/*

Flexmr. (2021). The Big Five Personality. *Blog.flexmr.net: https://blog. flexmr.net/ocean-personality-types*

Greenleaf, R. K. (1991). The Servant as Leader. Indianapolis, IN: The Robert K. Greenleaf Center. Jaccard, J. & Jacoby, J. (2010). *Theory construction and model-building skills.* New York, N.Y.: The Guilford Press.

Heifetz, R., Grashow, A., & Linsky, M. (2009). The practice of adaptive leadership: *Tools and tactics for changing your organization and the world.* Boston, MA: Harvard.

Herschel, A. (2021). Quotable Quote. *Goodreads.com: https://www. goodreads.com/quotes/231630-morally-speaking-there-is-no-limit-to- the-concern-one*

Jaccard, J & Jacoby, J. (2010). *Theory construction and model-building skills.* New York, N.Y.: The Guilford Press.

Kegan, R. and Lahey, L. (2001). *The real reason people won't change.* Cambridge, MA: Harvard Business Review.

Kennedy, John F. (2020). Direction. *Brainyquote.com: https://www. brainyquote.com/search_results?q=John+F.+Kennedy*

King, Martin, L., Jr. (1968). "The Drum Major Instinct." Sermon. Ebenezer Baptist Church, Atlanta, GA.

Kramer, Gary L. and Swing, Randy L. (Eds). 2010. Higher Education Assessments. Rowman & Littlefield: New York.

Middaugh, M. F. (2011). *Planning and assessment in higher education: Demonstrating institutional effectiveness.* John Wiley & Sons.

Miza, D. (2020). Dia Mirza Quotes. *BrainyQuote.com: https://www. brainyquote.com/authors/dia-mirza-quotes*

Northouse, Peter G. (2015). Leadership: Theory and practice (7th ed.). SAGE Publications, Inc.

Ritchie, A. L. (2011). Black History Month Feature/ Vernon Franklin: A Purposeful Life. *Chronicle.pitt.edu: https://www.chronicle.pitt.edu/story/black-history-month-featurevernon-franklin-purposeful-life*

Rost, J. (1993). *Leadership for the twenty-first century*. Westport, CT: Praeger Publishers.

Rozwell, C. & Adnams, S. (2019). Maverick* Research: Embrace Inclusion to Improve Team Performance. Gartner, Inc.

Schein, E. H. (1998). Organizational culture and leadership. San Francisco: Jossey-Bass.

Seibold, M., & Gamble, K. (2015). Capacity, commitment, and culture: The 3 Cs of staff development in a learning organization. *Psychiatric rehabilitation journal, 38*(3), 286.

Snowden, David J., & Boone, Mary E. (2022). A Leader's framework for Decision Making. *Harvard Business Review: https://hbr.org/2007/11/a-leaders-framework-for-decision-making/*

CHAPTER QUOTE REFERENCES

Blanchard, K. (202). SuccessStory. *Successstory.com: https://successstory.com/quote/kenneth-blanchard*

Corey, Irwin. (2020). Direction. *Brainyquote.com: https://www.brainyquote.com/search_results?q=Irwin+Corey*

Drucker, Peter. (2021). Vantage Circle Blog. Blog.vantagecircle.com: *https://blog.vantagecircle.com/quotes-for-training-employees/*

Garvey, Marcus. (2020). Culture Quotes. *Brainyquote.com: https://www.brainyquote.com/topics/culture-quotes*

Haaland, Deb. (2022). Sustainability Quotes. *Brainyquote.com:* https://www.brainyquote.com/quotes/deb_haaland_1123125

Kouly, Michael. (2016). Beyond Leadership. *Michaelkouly.com: https://www.michaelkouly.com/michael-kouly-blog/michael-kouly-quotes*

Linney, Laura. (2022). Authors. *BrainyQuote.com: https://www.brainyquote.com/quotes/laura_linney_453015*

Mark 2:22, (2011). BibleGateway. *Biblegateway.com: https://www.biblegateway.com/passage/?search=mark+2%3A22&version=NIV*

Moliere, (2015). ForbesQuotes. *Forbes.com: https://www.forbes.com/quotes/6902/*

Monet, Claude. (2022). Reflection Quotes. *AZ Quotes.com: https://www.azquotes.com/quotes/topics/reflection.html*

Rohn, Jim. (2020). Direction. *BrainyQuote.com: https://www.brainyquote.com/topics/direction-quotes*

Schweitzer, Albert. (2021). Purpose. *BrainyQuote.com: https://www.brainyquote.com/topics/purpose-quotes*

Shaw, George Bernard. (2022). Change. BrainyQuote.com: *https://www.brainyquote.com/quotes/george_bernard_shaw_386923*

Socrates. (2021). Socrates. *The Health Session: https://thehealthsessions.com/transformative-quotes-about-change/*

Socrates. (2020). Socrates. *Brainyquote.com: https://www.brainyquote.com/search_results?q=sorcrates*

Socrates. (2015). The Wise. *Brockington.leics.sch.uk: http://www.brockington.leics.sch.uk/wp-content/uploads/2015/04/Wise2.pdf*

Stepanek, Mattie. (2022). Collaboration Quotes. *BrainyQuote.com: https://www.brainyquote.com/topics/collaboration-quotes*

CONTACT INFORMATION FOR CONSULTATIONS,
PRESENTATIONS, AND WORKSHOPS

EMAIL:
VERNONF@PITT.EDU

FACEBOOK:
HTTPS://WWW.FACEBOOK.COM/VERNON.
FRANKLIN.9/

LINKEDIN:
HTTPS//WWW.LINKEDIN.COM/IN/VERNON-
FRANKLIN-ED-D-0B76447/

www.ingramcontent.com/pod-product-compliance
Lightning Source LLC
Chambersburg PA
CBHW070800290326
41931CB00011BA/2085